26 July 94

To My Darling, Beth
I love you very much.
Your Bill

GOLF
FOR
WOMEN

BEVERLY LEWIS

Photographs and illustrations by Ken Lewis

CRESCENT BOOKS
NEW YORK • AVENEL, NEW JERSEY

CLB 3040
© 1992 Colour Library Books Ltd., Godalming, Surrey, England
This 1993 edition published by Crescent Books,
distributed by Outlet Book Company, Inc., a Random House Company
34 Engelhard Avenue, Avenel, New Jersey 07001
Printed and bound in Italy
ISBN 0 517 07296 3
8 7 6 5 4 3 2 1

Contents

Introduction

A high proportion of golfers are women, and so it seems inappropriate that so few instruction books on golf are written either by women or for women. Consequently, I hope that this book will go some way towards correcting this imbalance.

Whilst not wishing to hint or suggest in any way that male teachers are not suitable or qualified to teach women, I do believe that it is only a woman professional golfer who can fully appreciate the usual lack of strength that the average female beginner experiences. Therefore, a female teacher is able to understand better and solve the problems that are going to arise with the less gifted and weakest of women through to the more athletic pupil.

Compared to any man, be he office or manual worker, women have less innate strength, so we must rely on good technique and rhythm rather than sheer power if we wish to play golf well. We must also make full use of the clubs we use, perhaps relying more on fairway woods than the unforgiving long irons in our set. The short game is one area where we can compete on equal terms, and so all readers will benefit from that section of this book.

I do feel that the average male golfer could also improve with the advice contained in these pages. In the many pro-ams I have played with men, they are quick to point out that they feel they can relate better to the way a top class female professional plays, than to the game of a male professional. So I would be surprised, not to say disappointed, if male golfers, should they happen to read this book, do not improve their golfing prowess.

It would be fair to say that the majority of golfers are in the middle to high handicap range, and this book is primarily aimed at them and, of course, the total beginner. However, none of us ever masters the game to the extent that we can learn nothing more about how to improve our swing, our shot making, or the ability to correct our faults. I hope through reading this book, all three will be possible, so there is something to be gained for those of you in the lower handicap divisions as well.

No matter how many books you read, or lessons you take, you will only improve with practice. This does not necessarily mean spending three to four hours a day practising, as quality of work is often better than just quantity. Most movements in golf have to be learnt, and then kept under constant review to be performed at their best. So I hope that you are able to practise what I advocate throughout the book. If your club does not have a practice ground, try to visit a local driving range, or perhaps fit a net in your garden. It is much easier when starting to play or making major changes to practise first off the course, where you will not be so concerned about where the ball is going.

The marvellous thing about the game of golf is that one is never too old to take it up. It does not require supreme fitness, like tennis does, but instead offers gentle exercise that is good for you physically and which relaxes you mentally.

If it is any comfort, I did not start playing golf until I was about eighteen years old, sadly past the age when one is content to mimic the best players. My first round was played on a local nine-hole course, with hired clubs, and in open-toed sandals! After that one round, I was totally hooked on the game. Eventually I bought my first half set of clubs, and a season ticket for the municipal golf course. Two or three years later, I joined my first private golf club, and considered it a great privilege to play in such tranquil surroundings. Although I had a certain athletic and sporting ability, I found golf to be a demanding, infuriating, but supremely satisfying game. I have always had to practise hard, not necessarily immediately reaping the rewards I thought justified but eventually seeing that work pay off. I enjoyed practising as an amateur, but as a professional tournament player I had to discipline myself to practise when I really would have preferred to relax. Golf is your hobby and should not become a chore, but without some effort you will not get the full benefit of this book. So I hope you enjoy the practice as well as the reading.

All the instruction in this book has been written for the golfer playing the game right-handed, so my apologies to those of you who stand the opposite side of the ball and who, I'm afraid, will have to translate right for left, and so on.

Chapter 1

Starting out

This chapter introduces you to the game of golf, dealing first with a few important points on club selection, and giving you some good ideas on what it is you should be trying to achieve in the swing.

With the help of the clockface analogy I do believe you'll find golf an easier game to learn and play. I have explained in great detail why good posture is needed and its effect on the swing — this is one area that we women seem to find most difficult. The address and ball position is fully explained because if you do not get the stationary part of the game correct, then a good swing is hard to achieve.

In building your swing, if you start by getting the half swing correct you'll find a full swing develops quite easily. Most of us have swing faults, but by recognising them sooner rather than later you can correct them. So the last section of this book highlights some of the most common swing faults, and offers simple remedies.

Selecting the right equipment...
ladies' versus men's clubs

I feel it is important to mention something about equipment before anything to do with the swing. I have seen many ladies using clubs that are making golf even more difficult than necessary. So often a lady will start the game inheriting her husband's old clubs. While it is advisable to find out if you like the game before spending a fortune on equipment, men's clubs will prove to be totally unsuitable for the vast majority of women to start with. It is better to buy a ladies' 6 or 7 iron, either new or second hand, or borrow a female friend's clubs. Once you know that you are going to take the game seriously, then either add to the single club you have already purchased, or look for a decent set or half set.

Why ladies' clubs?

There are three main reasons why you should have ladies' clubs, and these are to do with swing weight, shaft flex, and grip size.

1 The swing weight is a method of referring to how heavy the club feels when it is swung, and ladies' clubs range from about C0-C8 (see club weight table). If you use men's clubs, you will more than likely find them too heavy to control. The essence of the golf swing is to control the clubhead and if you swing too heavy a club it will control you. It may well be that if you are stronger than the average woman, and have perhaps played tennis or squash to a good standard, you might well be strong enough from the start to use men's clubs. But even this category of player would do better to start with ladies' clubs, then perhaps progress to a man's set.

2 The shaft on ladies' clubs is quite flexible, which helps to promote clubhead speed and thus, ultimately, to improve the distance the ball goes. Until you can generate so much power that the slightly longer and firmer men's shaft will give you additional control without sacrificing distance, then always use ladies' 'L' shafts. Indeed, some older and less athletic men derive great benefit from using ladies' clubs, since the shorter, whippy shaft and lighter weight enables them to control the club and gain extra distance without more effort.

3 The grips on ladies' clubs are smaller than those on men's, which usually make them easier to hold. However, ladies with large hands and long fingers may find larger grips help them to grip the club correctly. If the grip is the right size, then the tip of the middle finger of your left hand should

SWING WEIGHT	C0-C5	C6-C8	C9-D2
SHAFT	L	L or R	R
CATEGORY OF PLAYER	The unathletic beginner and average lady player. The light swing weight is easy to control.	The stronger lady beginner and more athletic player who has developed reasonable control and clubhead speed. Some men may find clubs with L shafts easier to control and that the more flexible shaft promotes club-head speed.	The very strong lady player and average man. The firmer shaft allied to increased clubhead weight pro-motes control and distance for the player with well developed hand action and club-head speed.

not quite meet the base of the thumb.

Keep these three major points in mind when you purchase your clubs, and you should buy the correct equipment. More specific details about the variety of golf clubs available are covered in a later chapter.

It will help you to understand the following swing instruction in this book if you know what different parts of the club are called.

Shaft

Toe

Face

Leading Edge

Hosel

Shank

Whipping

Face

Toe

Insert

Sole Plate

Heel

The concept of the swing . . .

Before I describe the grip, stance, and swing, I feel that it is most important that you have a good idea of what you are trying to achieve when you swing. Many golfers swing the club without a clear idea or plan of what they are trying to do. In the very early stages of learning the game, there are so many new movements and facts to absorb that the total beginner could be forgiven for not paying too much attention to the swing path direction, or clubface alignment. In the beginning coping with gripping the club and getting a reasonable address position seem the most monumental tasks, and concerning oneself with clubhead direction seems just too much to take on board. However, it is never too early to visualize what you are trying to do.

The clock face analogy

I want to introduce to you what I believe is a very simple way of analyzing the golf swing. I continually use the clock face analogy in my teaching, and have never yet found any one who cannot relate to it.

Imagine that when you *address the ball* (stand with it in front of you), it is in the middle of a clock face on the ground. You are standing at 6.00 o'clock, with 3.00 o'clock on your right, and 9.00 o'clock on your left. A line drawn from 3.00 to 9.00 represents a line through the ball to the target, called the target line. As you swing the clubhead away, it will move towards 3.00 o'clock for a short distance, then as your body continues to turn, the clubhead will swing upwards between 3.00 and 4.00 o'clock. Ideally it will swing down on a very similar path, and approach the ball from about 3.30, strike the ball whilst it is moving towards 9.00 o'clock, then travel towards 8.00 as your body turns to face the target.

● At impact the clubface must be square to the target to produce a straight shot.
● If it faces to the right, the ball will curve to the right.
● If it faces to the left, the ball will curve to the left.
● The area between the target line and you, is called inside, and that beyond the target line is outside. It is important that the clubhead approaches the ball from inside the target line to gain maximum power, distance and accuracy. When the club approaches from outside the line, the ball is given a glancing blow, and much of the power in the swing is wasted.

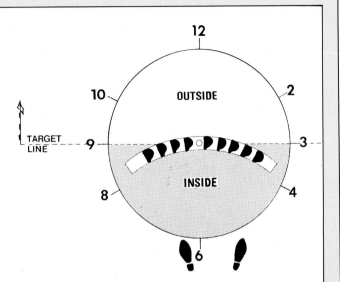

When the clubhead moves in the correct manner, it is on an *in to in* swing path. If it swings more from 4.00 to 10.00 o'clock, this is called *in to out*, and more from 2.00 to 8.00 o'clock is called *out to in*.

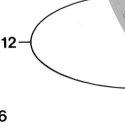

This is as much detail as I wish to go into at this point, but I will be referring to the clock face analogy throughout this book. Further information and explanation of the swing will be included later, mainly in the section on slicing and hooking (page 90). But for now, learn how to hit the ball correctly, and the above will certainly help.

The correct grip...
a solid foundation to a good swing

The main purpose of the grip is to return the club-face squarely to the ball at impact, without any undue independent manipulation or contrivance. So, if you grip the club correctly to start with, at impact the hands will naturally return to the correct position, and the ball should fly fairly straight. Unfortunately, for many beginners, what seems the most natural and comfortable grip is far from the right one. To start with you may find the correct grip feels strange, and will be tempted to return to what *feels* ideal. This really does epitomize golf. So often a player will do the most comfortable thing, only to discover she has been cultivating a fault. So for those of you who have played the game for some time, but are about to discover that something as basic as your grip has been wrong, please be patient and persevere with any changes that have to be made. I would say that a grip change is perhaps the hardest thing to cope with, but if you are determined to improve your game, it will, without doubt, be worthwhile.

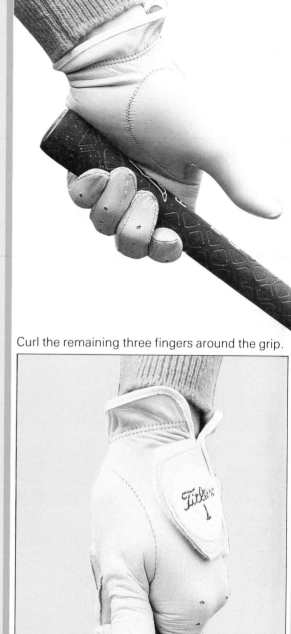

Curl the remaining three fingers around the grip.

With the clubface square to the target, begin to assemble the grip. The back of your left hand should face the target with the club lying diagonally across your hand, resting in the crook of the index finger. The end or butt must lie under the fleshy pad at the heel of your hand, allowing about a quarter of an inch of the club to protrude.

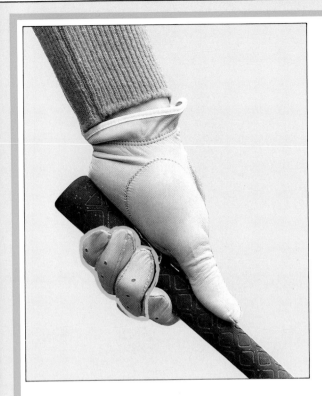

Place your thumb just to the right of the top of the grip. As you look down you will see a 'V' formed between thumb and index finger. Be sure that there is no gap at the base of this 'V', as it must form a solid support at the top of the swing. The 'V' must point to the right side of your face, and you should be able to see two to two-and-a-half knuckles. Do not stretch your thumb down the shaft, as this will tighten up the forearm muscles.

When viewed from *face on,* the end of the thumb and the middle knuckle of the index finger are about level. The left hand is very much a combination of fingers and palm forming the grip, which gives a feeling of solidity. Grip pressure is applied mainly by the last three fingers.

To test if your grip is correct, hold the club up in front of you, and uncurl the last three fingers and release the thumb. The club should balance quite easily under the heel of the hand and across the index finger.

The correct grip

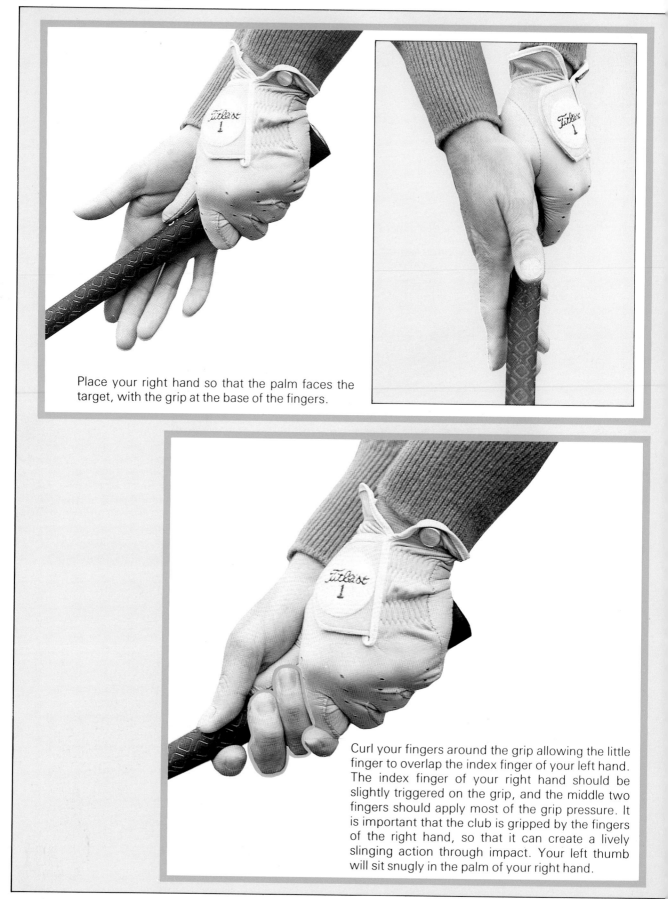

Place your right hand so that the palm faces the target, with the grip at the base of the fingers.

Curl your fingers around the grip allowing the little finger to overlap the index finger of your left hand. The index finger of your right hand should be slightly triggered on the grip, and the middle two fingers should apply most of the grip pressure. It is important that the club is gripped by the fingers of the right hand, so that it can create a lively slinging action through impact. Your left thumb will sit snugly in the palm of your right hand.

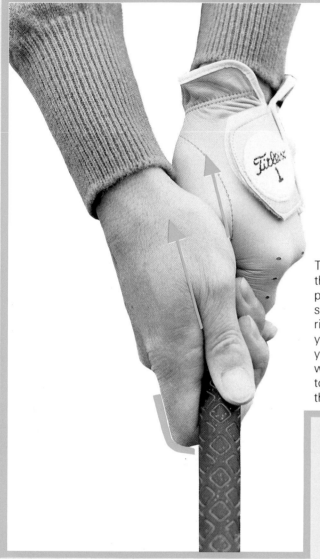

The 'V' between thumb and index finger points to the region of your right ear, and should be virtually parallel to the 'V' of your left hand. Again there should be no gap at the base of the 'V', and your right thumb sits just left of centre on the grip. If your left thumb is sitting correctly in the palm of your right hand, when viewed from face on you will see little or nothing of the left thumb. It is clear to see that the triggered right index finger sits at the side of, rather than underneath, the grip.

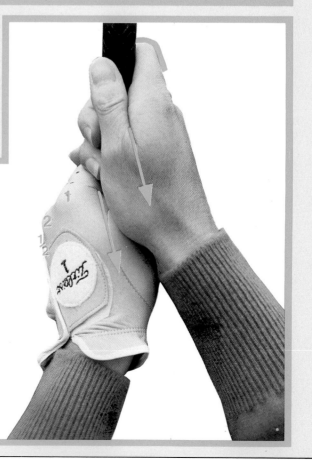

When you hold the club up in front of you, check the points that I have detailed.
- Two to two-and-a-half knuckles of the left hand are visible.
- Both 'V's are parallel and pointing between the right side of your face and your right shoulder.
- Your left thumb rests in the hollow of your right palm.
- Your right index finger is slightly triggered at the *side* of the grip.

The correct grip

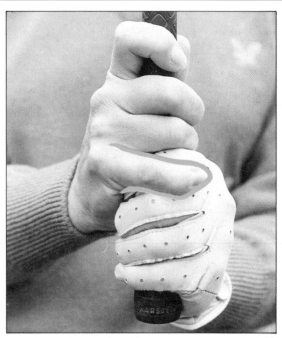

A variation of this grip is to overlap the little finger between the index finger and middle finger of the left hand.

I use and recommend the overlap or Vardon grip, where the little finger of the right hand overlaps the left index finger. I prefer this grip because it makes my hands a more complete unit and also keeps all of my left hand on the grip, which promotes better control.

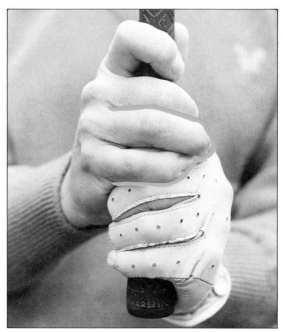

A word of warning: if, like me, you have small hands, make sure that, if you choose to overlap between the two fingers of your left hand, you do not pull the right ring finger into an overlapping position as well. This finger *must* remain on the grip, so make that your guide as to just where you rest your right little finger.

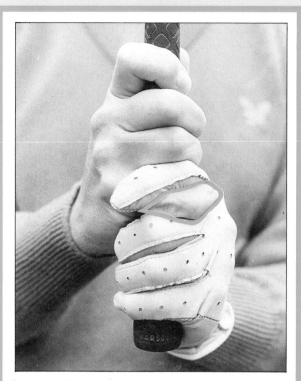

Some golfers choose to interlock their right little finger and left index finger. I personally do not favour or teach this as I believe it denies some authority in the left hand. However, since Jack Nicklaus is perhaps the greatest exponent of this grip, it would be quite wrong of me to say it is not the grip to use, I would suggest you try the overlapping grip before giving this one a try.

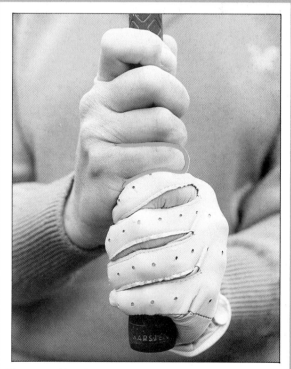

The two-handed or baseball grip may well suit beginners or ladies with small hands. It allows the whole of each hand to be placed on the grip, thereby giving extra control. If you decide to use this grip, be certain that the two hands are butted firmly against each other, as any gap allowed to develop will encourage the hands to work separately, rather than as one unit. I started with this grip, but I do feel that my game improved when I changed to the overlapping grip.

The correct grip

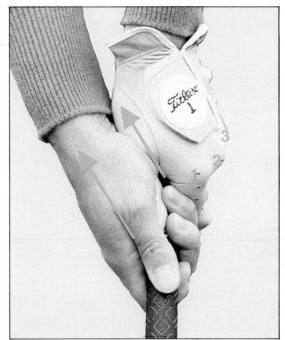

The strong grip

A *strong* grip refers to the position of the hands on the club, and not their tightness. In a strong grip the hands are turned too much to the right, so that three or even four knuckles of the left hand are visible. The two 'V's' point too much towards the right shoulder, or even outside it. The right hand starts to grip the club too much in the palm, instead of the fingers. At impact the hands will tend to return into a more neutral position, and this has the effect of closing the clubface, producing shots that go to the left.

The most common bad grip

This ugly example of a grip unfortunately crops up all too often. For many a beginner it is the most natural and comfortable way to hold the club, but please, if you recognize this as the same or very similar to your grip, change it immediately. Neither hand has a redeeming feature to offer, and each is placed on the grip so there is absolutely no chance of them working in harmony. The hands will fight each other to find the correct action, and I can assure you that you will *never* play to your maximum potential with such a monster as this. If it takes you weeks to get used to the correct grip, then so be it, but do not even try to persevere with this grip.

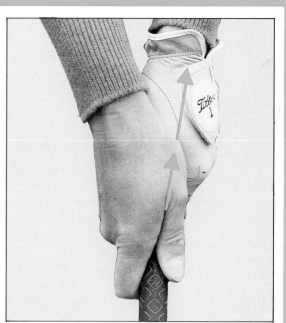

The weak grip

The *weak* grip refers to the position in which the hands are placed on the grip, and not grip pressure. In the weak grip the hands are turned too much to the left, so that barely one knuckle of the left hand is visible. Often with this grip the shaft lies up the middle of the left hand, rather than under the pad at the heel. The two 'V's point towards the chin or even to the left of it, and both thumbs are too much to the left of the grip. As explained in the strong grip, the hands tend to return to a more neutral position at impact, and in this instance they will produce an open clubface at impact, making the ball go to the right.

The correct grip for you

I have shown you how to adopt what is technically the correct grip, but as I said at the beginning of this section, the purpose of the grip is to return the clubface to a square position at impact. While to start with you may benefit from having a grip that shows two-and-a-half to three knuckles of the left hand, and both 'V's' pointing between the right ear and right shoulder, as you progress, and develop good hand action, you may need to adjust the grip to a more neutral position, with both hands a little more to the left on the grip with two to two-and-a-half knuckles showing, depending on the flight of the ball.

Grip pressure

It is difficult to be exact about grip pressure. Far more of my pupils grip the club too tightly than grip it too loosely. You need to grip it just tight enough to have control, but not so tightly that you tense up the forearm and hand muscles. You may well have seen athletes prior to their race moving gently from one leg to the other, keeping the thigh and calf muscles relaxed, as they know that it is in this state that muscles work best. Grip the club so that your hands feel firm but light. They will tighten up a little during the swing, so if you start with them tight, they will be far too tight and tense as the swing progresses. As a rough guide, if there were a scale of 1-5, with 1 being loose, and 5 being tight, the grip pressure is about $3\text{-}3\frac{1}{2}$.

Good posture...
why women find this difficult

During teaching, I find certain faults arise more frequently than others, and one of the most common, especially for ladies, is wrong posture. Unlike other golf authors, I am covering this subject before aiming and ball position, because I want its importance in the game to register very early in the learning process. In your address position, you are pre-determining, to a very large extent, the shape and direction of the swing. This is why golf teachers spend a lot of time checking and correcting it.

So what is correct posture? The best place to observe a player's posture is by standing to their right looking towards the target, called standing *behind* them. You can then notice the angles of the back and legs, the weight distribution, and the position of the head. You can also see the distance between player and ball, which is directly related to posture. Correct posture is important because, first of all, it creates space in which your arms can hang, and ultimately swing. It ensures that your body will not impede your arms at all. It promotes the correct body action which blends with the arms swinging. It will also position you the correct distance from the ball.

There are three main reasons for poor posture in women golfers. The first two also apply to men, since they involve two well-known adages in golf: 'feel like you are sitting on a shooting stick', and 'keep your head down', both of which lead to bad posture.

1 If you adopt a posture where you feel like you are sitting on a shooting stick, your weight is placed predominantly on your heels. No athletic sport, where leg action is important, can be played with most of the weight on the heels, since the legs are not mobile enough. A tennis player about to receive serve resting back on her heels would never be able to move quickly enough. I am not suggesting that we need to move around as much as tennis players do, but golf, if it is to be played well, must be considered an athletic sport.

2 Keeping your head down is probably the advice that the majority of people learn first and misinterpret most. If you start with your head down, your chin will be tucked on your chest which will most certainly restrict your backswing and throughswing. Mobility is essential in golf, and to restrict your backswing in this manner is counter productive, and will lead to neck problems. I have told many more pupils to keep their heads up, than I have ever told to keep them down, and I suspect I am not the only teacher to make that claim. The answer is to keep your head *up* and eyes *down,* focussing on the ball.

3 The third reason for bad posture applies to women only. I believe it dates back to training when young to attain a good walking posture. This involved keeping an erect spine, with the shoulders back and seat tucked in. Correct golf posture requires that as you bend forward your seat must go out behind you, a complete anathema to many women golfers.

Consequently, when addressing the ball they keep their seats tucked in, which means their hip bones are pulled forward. In this position it is *impossible* for the hips to *turn* as they should in the swing. Instead, the hips slide laterally to the right and then the left, which prevents the swing developing power and good direction. Men can sometimes make a good swing with little hip turn, but this is because they generally have narrower hips than women, and they can still turn their shoulders sufficiently.

It is very useful to go through the following drill with the help of a full length mirror or patio doors in which you can see your reflection. Perform the drill at first without a ball, because if you have been standing either too close or too far from the ball, you will be very much inclined to set your posture to suit the ball position. Practise without the ball to begin with, so that you are not inhibited, and so that you get some idea of where the ball *should* be to suit your physique.

With a medium iron, perhaps the 6, stand erect with your feet together, your arms out in front of you, and hands at waist height. Do not stretch your arms away from you, but keep the area between shoulder and elbow lightly touching the sides of your body, and have the club virtually horizontal.

Lower the clubhead to the ground by bending forward from the hip bones. As this happens, your shoulders will come forward, and your seat will move out behind you as a counter balance.

Place your feet slightly apart and flex your knees a comfortable amount. You can now clearly see that correct posture results in very definite angles, with the back fairly straight but angled forward, and the knees flexed. Your spine has to remain fairly straight, but your hip bones should be tilted back a little, forming a very slight hollow at the base of your spine. Do not pull your hip bones forward so that your seat is tucked in. The weight is not completely on heels or toes, but distributed between the heels and balls of your feet. This will enable your legs and feet to work quite actively in the swing. Your head should be up and eyes down looking at the ball. Basically, your head remains as an extension of the spine, much as it was above left. With the 6 iron, there should be a gap between the butt end of the club and your thighs about a fist wide. There should be an angle between your arms and the shaft. It is said that the left arm and shaft should form a straight line, and whilst this is true when seen from in front, from the side there must be an angle.

Good posture

Posture will change with different clubs. Using a wedge, my back angles forward a little more, my hands are closer to my thighs and, due to the shorter shaft, naturally I will be standing closer to the ball. My weight is a *little* more towards the balls of my feet than for a medium iron.

With the driver, my spine is a little more erect, my hands are further from my thighs than with the 6 iron and, due to the length of the shaft, I am standing further away from the ball. The weight is a *little* more towards the heels than for an iron.

Correct posture dictates the distance you stand from the ball. If your posture remains unchanged, when, for example, the driver is grounded, the wedge will be in the air. This means that you have to bend forward until the head of the wedge is grounded. This spot naturally occurs closer to your feet.

Good posture

These are two horrors, but sadly show a very common error. In both pictures my weight is too much on my heels. My seat has been tucked in, causing my hip bones to tilt forward. My back is too rounded and, in the left picture, my arms are very close to my body, leaving me no space in which to swing. Having realized this, and in order to create some space, in the picture above I have arched my wrists upwards. This does in fact create a little space in which the arms can swing, but that is of no consequence as the wrists are unable to work correctly.

A less common error, stretching for the ball, tends to promote a stiff-legged address position. There is certainly enough space here in which to swing, but overstretching stops the body and legs working correctly, and loss of balance is inevitable.

Many more players stand too close to the ball than stand too far away. If, after finding the correct posture, you feel you are standing further from the ball than before, you may feel that you are stretching. But, remember, all feelings in golf are relative to what you were doing previously. Practise swinging from this new position without the ball, and you will find that you have much more space in which to swing your arms, and you will soon get used to the new position.

Aiming the swing and ball position

Golfers tend to underestimate the importance of this aspect of the game. They believe that the 'secret' of being a good player is how you swing the club. But your swing is affected by how you *set up* (address the ball). If you aim and align yourself and the clubface in the wrong direction, you will have to make compensations in your swing in order to hit the ball towards the target. Many people play in this manner, but they almost certainly never reach what would have been, for them, their highest standard of play. They are feeding their fault instead of starving it. Try to eradicate as many errors as possible, first from your grip and set-up. This will lead, in turn, perhaps eventually rather than instantly, to a far more consistent standard of golf.

Aiming the swing and ball position are interrelated. Incorrect ball positioning can throw the shoulders out of line, and shoulder alignment is most influential on the clubhead swing path and, consequently, the direction in which the ball flies.

The vast majority of golfers that I teach have an error in their alignment and ball position. It can be difficult to visualize the correct ball position. In teaching, I often stand exactly in my pupils' footprints and address the ball, then send them round to view the set-up from the 'teacher's' side. The fault then becomes obvious and they concede that what they thought they were doing, and what they were doing, were two different things. Why should aiming your swing in the correct direction be so difficult? Just think about it. To hit a golf ball, you stand sideways to, rather than facing, the target, so that you do not even have the target in your peripheral vision when you hit the ball. You stand several inches to the left of the target line, and you then have to hit sideways. Compare this to a marksman. If you asked him to hold his gun at arm's length, stand sideways and then hit his target, he too would find aiming more difficult. Aim and alignment are things that the best players in the world constantly practise and check. If you get it wrong at this stage, it spells trouble for the future.

Change of ball position for change of strike
Understanding what you are doing will make ball positioning easier, so I want to give you a simple explanation of how and why the ball position alters.

As the club is swung towards the ball, it descends, briefly travels parallel to the ground, then starts to ascend after the ball has been struck. To strike the ball correctly with an iron, the clubhead should be descending. This will impart backspin which, apart from getting the ball airborne, helps control the shot. Therefore, the ball needs to be positioned just before the lowest point in the swing, which is called the *base of the arc*.

To get the best results with fairway woods, the ball should be struck when the clubhead is at the base of the arc, travelling virtually parallel to the ground. Therefore, the ball should be positioned a little further to the left on the target line than for iron shots.

To get maximum distance from a driver, the ball is best struck when the clubhead is *just* starting to ascend, so it should be positioned a little further to the left than for fairway woods.

The base of the arc will vary from player to player, mainly depending on how much leg, hand and arm action is used. At the beginner's stage it is better to err by having the ball too central, rather than too far forward. My suggestions of distances in the following sequence should be acceptable for most people, but you may need to experiment to some extent.

Here is a system which will make correct lining up and ball position more simple. Practise it, even in your own garden, and you will soon feel comfortable in the correct position, and it will become second nature to you.

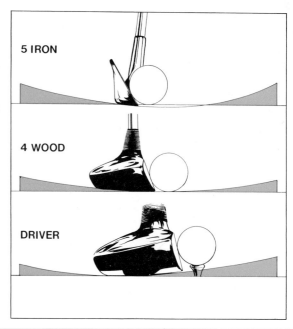

5 IRON

4 WOOD

DRIVER

2 Using a 5 or 6 iron, stand with your feet together with the inside of your left heel opposite the back of the ball (the side of the ball that is struck by the club).

1

Stand behind the ball, and pick out an intermediate target a leaf perhaps, about a yard ahead of your ball and between it and the target.

4 Now move your left foot approximately its own width to the left. This should position the back of the ball about 3 inches or two balls' width inside the left heel.

3

Position the clubface so that it is at right angles to an imaginary line from your ball to the intermediate target. When you stand with your feet together, it is likely that your shoulders, hips and knees will be parallel to the target line, but check anyway.

Aiming the swing and ball position

Move your right foot about 9 inches to the right, letting your weight fall equally on the inside of each foot. These distances will vary from player to player depending on height and swing characteristics. For the longer irons you must move your *right* foot progressively just a *little* more to the right, whereas for shorter clubs you move it progressively less to the right. So for all normal iron shots, the ball stays in the same relationship to the left foot, and the right foot alters the width of the stance. Both feet are angled outwards a little.

Other points to be noticed from this angle are: the straight line formed by my left arm and the shaft; the back of my left hand is ahead of the ball; the shaft slopes towards the target; both eyes are behind the ball; my knees are bent very slightly towards each other; my right shoulder is lower than my left.

In the correct set-up, lines drawn across my shoulders, knees, hips, and feet would all be parallel to the target line. This gives me the best chance of striking the ball while the clubhead is moving towards the target, most essential for a good shot. It is a mistaken idea that the shoulders point at the target, they point parallel left of it. My eyes are also parallel to the target line, which gives me the true perspective of the shot. While my left arm is straight, there is just a little give in my right arm, with the elbow pointing towards my right hip bone. Also, you can just see some of my left arm. One can liken the set-up to railway lines, with the ball and clubhead on the far rail, and the body on the near one.

If the ball is played too far forward (too far to the left) in the stance, it tends to pull the shoulder line into an open position. A line across the shoulders will aim left, rather than parallel left of the target line. This will almost certainly result in the club-head travelling to the left of the target, out to in, at impact.

If the ball is played too far back (too far to the right) in the stance it sets the shoulders into a closed position. A line across them would aim right of parallel. This can result in the clubhead travelling too much to the right of the target, in to out, at impact, but can cause the player to compensate incorrectly and result in a swing from out to in.

Aiming the swing and ball position

When using the wedge, your right foot will not be so far to the right. The ball looks central in my stance, but it remains in the same position in relation to my left foot. The left foot is placed in an open position ie a line cross my toes aims left of parallel to the target. The left foot is angled open a little, but the right foot is square to the target line. What *has* altered is my weight distribution, and now there is more weight on my left foot than on my right, maybe in a ratio of 60/40. This changes several aspects of the set-up compared to the 6 iron. My left eye is more in line with the ball; my shoulders are nearer the horizontal; both hands are ahead of the ball; the shaft is sloping more towards the target.

Since shots with a fairway wood must be struck when the clubhead is at the base of the arc, the ball should be a little nearer the left foot than for irons. Adopt the same address procedure, but only move the left foot about 2 inches to the left, with the weight evenly distributed. This should enable you to sweep the ball from the turf, rather than strike down on it. Compared to the 6 iron set-up, my eyes are further behind the ball; my right shoulder is lower than my left; and the back of my left hand is about level with the front of the ball.

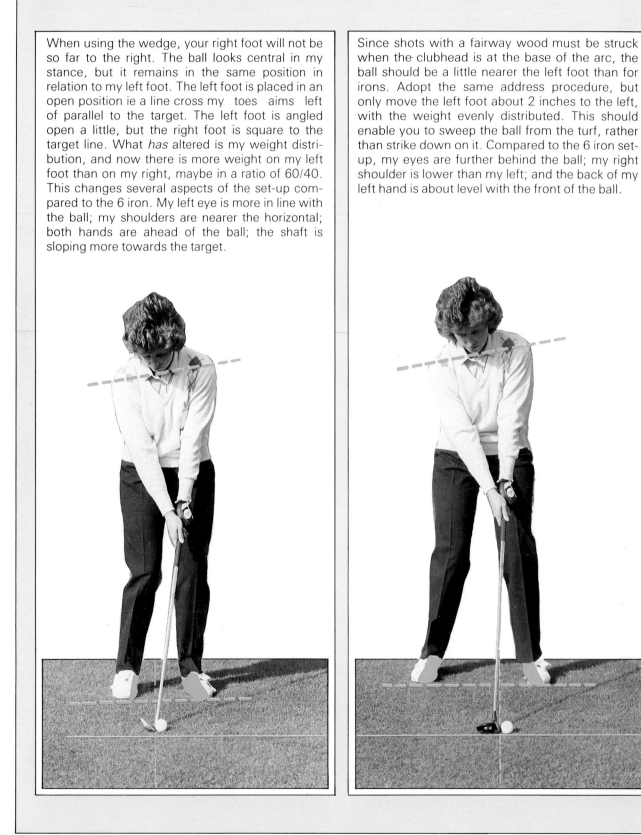

As shots with the driver should be struck when the clubhead is *just* starting to ascend, the ball needs to be positioned a little nearer the left foot than for fairway woods. Adopt the same set-up procedure again, but only move the left foot about 1 inch to the left. As you move your right foot, allow a little more weight to settle on that side, maybe 60/40 in favour of the right. The stance should now be at its widest. Do not overdo it, the space between the insides of my heels is just narrower than my shoulders. This will vary from player to player, depending on physique, but you must have a firm base on which to make your most aggressive swing. Other points to note: my eyes are now well behind the ball; my right shoulder is very much lower than my left; the back of my left hand is about level with the centre of the ball; my right knee is bent slightly inwards.

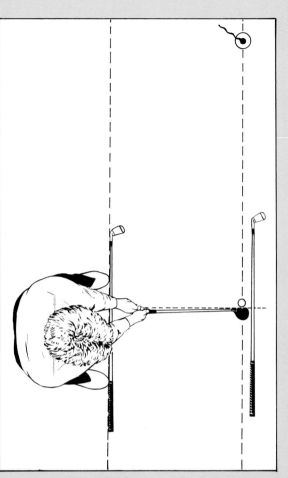

Practise with clubs on the ground, laid parallel to the target line. Perhaps also use a third club, placed at right angles to these two, and in line with the back of the ball. Try practising in front of a mirror or patio doors. Make use of any square tiles or paving slabs in or around your house to help you achieve squareness. When you are playing a friendly game (not a competition) ask your playing partner to check your alignment. The main point to remember is that your shoulder line is the most influential, and a club across them should be *parallel* to and *left* of the target line, *not* pointing at the target.

The ball positions recommended are for normal, or straight, shots from a flat lie. Changes are made when trying to shape the shot, and from sloping lies, but these will be dealt with in a later chapter. If your iron shots are not struck crisply, experiment with the ball position. Until such time as you are able to blend good hand, arm, and leg action into your swing, you may need to play the ball just a little more centrally than in the photographs, which should ensure the correct ball-turf contact.

The half swing... getting the fundamentals right

The essence of the golf swing is to control the clubhead which, to a certain extent, involves strength, but it also involves good technique. If you are trying golf as your first sporting activity, it is reasonable to expect a lack of physical strength. You may not, initially, possess quite enough strength to control the club in a full swing, so start with a half swing, where lack of power will not be too detrimental. Even those of you who feel you are fairly athletic, perhaps you have played squash, tennis or some other sport, would benefit from this section for, although it calls on little physical effort, what you learn in the half swing is the ground work for the full swing.

Many people have the wrong idea of how to hit the ball. It is not just a hand and arm swing. Every part of the body plays its role. Learn to incor-porate the correct movements of the hands, arms, body and legs. Once the half swing can quite readily be repeated, it is only a matter of extending it until you have the finished article — the full swing.

In Chapter 4 there are some exercises for strengthening the muscles for golf. Select one or two of the forearm exercises initially and repeat them as often as possible. Half swings themselves will build golfing muscles. You don't have to look like Popeye, with bulging muscles, to play the game well. Some of the best women golfers in the world, who hit the ball vast distances, are the most feminine-looking of sportswomen. So swing and exercise as much as you can, or indeed want to. After all, golf is your hobby, and it must not become a chore.

TARGET LINE

Address the ball, which is either sitting on a low tee or good cushion of grass and choke down a little on a 6 or 7 iron (move your hands down the grip). Leave a club lying on the ground just outside the ball, representing the target line. Imagine that your arms and shoulders form a triangle, with the club shaft an extension from the side formed by the left arm.

To start the backswing, move the left shoulder, left arm and shaft back (away from the target) together, until your hands are about level with your right thigh. At this point the triangle of the arms and shoulders has started to swing to the right, but the hands have remained passive. Even at this early stage the right hip has turned a little, and the left knee has started to flex inwards.

As the hands and arms continue to swing back they rotate slightly clockwise. At waist height the wrists have cocked quite a lot due to the swinging weight of the clubhead. The triangle has continued to turn, the shoulders are not yet at 90°, the right elbow has folded, so that it is starting to point towards the ground. The back of the left hand faces forwards, virtually parallel to the target line, and the left arm is comfortably straight. The right hip has continued to turn and the right knee

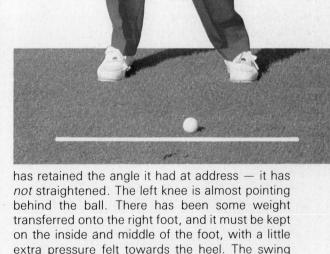

You can see that the clubhead has swung back towards 3.00 o'clock, but is just beginning to move towards 3.30. This is indicated by the fact it is no longer touching the target line. The clubhead is still quite close to the ground.

has retained the angle it had at address — it has *not* straightened. The left knee is almost pointing behind the ball. There has been some weight transferred onto the right foot, and it must be kept on the inside and middle of the foot, with a little extra pressure felt towards the heel. The swing has been made around a fixed point at the top of my spine. There is no suggestion of swaying to the right.

The half swing

From this angle you can see that the clubhead has continued to move inside towards the 4.00 o'clock position. The main point to check is that the leading edge of the clubface is 90° to the horizon and the toe of the club points skywards. This shows that my wrists have cocked correctly. If I were to turn my body and feet round now to face the camera, then ground the clubhead, I would be back in my address position. My spine has remained at the angle I set it at address.

The most common error at this point is for the clubface to be pointing towards the ground, so that the leading edge is less than 90° to the horizon, and the back of the left wrist faces towards the ground. To correct this fault, try to feel that your left arm rotates clockwise a little as you swing the clubhead upwards. At the moment it is rotating anti-clockwise, ie turning under.

If your hands and arms have rotated too much in a clockwise direction, the clubface will point skywards, and the leading edge will have passed beyond 90°. To correct this, keep your hands very passive at the start of the backswing, and try to feel as if you are swinging the clubhead upwards, not behind you.

Perhaps the easiest way to check your wrist ▶ action is to address the ball, then simply cock your wrists up in front of you until the club is just above the horizontal. Check that the leading edge is at 90°. Now swing your arms back, and you should be in the correct position (see page 35). Remember that the left wrist cocks in a sideways motion during the backswing. It does *not* hinge back on itself, and it does *not* bow, so that the left palm has moved towards the under side of the left forearm.

The half swing

Swing your *arms* down, and allow your wrists to uncock. While the most important part of the golf swing is impact, it is very difficult to check it as it happens so quickly. But in the early stages of learning, working without a ball, and ideally with the aid of a mirror, stop your swing at the base of the arc and check that the clubface is now looking directly towards the target. Try making several slow motion swings, stopping at impact. The back of your left wrist must remain firm, and must not collapse back on itself. Your weight should return from the right foot back towards, but not entirely on, the left foot, with the right knee flexing inwards, and the right heel just off the ground. The triangular pattern of the arms and shoulders is in evidence and the left hip is starting to turn out of the way.

The clubhead will have been swung back to the ball on a very similar path to the backswing and will approach the ball from just inside the target line, from the 3.30 direction. This should happen naturally if you do not try to use your upper body, particularly your right shoulder which throws the swing onto an outside path, more in the 2.00 to 8.00 o'clock direction. If you swing your *arms down* first, you will attack the ball from the inside. Notice that my shoulders at impact are virtually parallel to the target line.

As the throughswing develops beyond the point of impact, the hands and arms will continue to rotate anti-clockwise. By the time the hands are waist high, the toe of the club will point skywards, and the back of the right hand will be virtually parallel to the target line. The left arm will begin to fold with the elbow starting to point down towards the ground. The wrists have cocked upwards, but the back of the left wrist still remains firm and in line with the back of the left forearm. The shoulders have turned so that the triangular relationship still exists. The left hip has turned out of the way. The left knee is still a little flexed, with the weight towards the outside of the foot, and nearer the heel. The right knee now points ahead of the ball, and the right heel is completely off the ground. My head has started to rotate towards the target.

From this angle you can see how I have turned through the ball, but my body has been pulled through by my arms to face towards the target. The leading edge of the club is angled a little towards the ground, which shows that my hands have been working well. Try to reproduce this position. The clubface should not point even slightly towards the sky at this point. Since my body has turned through, the clubhead has been swung back to the inside towards 8.00 o'clock. I have retained the angle in which I set my spine at address.

The golf swing is not a series of positions, but one continuous movement. However, when learning the game, by checking your movements at certain points in the swing you can spot your mistakes and correct them. Practise the swing checking first of all the clubface position, then pay a little more attention to what you are physically doing. Progress to making the whole swing as one continuous movement, trying to accelerate the clubhead *through* the ball. Practise at first without a ball and concentrate very intently on a piece of grass as an imaginary ball. Then try to make the clubhead brush this on the way through. To strike an iron shot correctly, the clubhead must still be descending at the point of impact, so do not try to hit the ball *up* into the air. Be sure to hit down and through, taking a divot or some grass. Even at this stage, try to make the movement smooth and rhythmical, creating what is, in reality, a mini-swing in every sense.

The full swing ... just a matter of extending the half swing

If you can swing the club quite freely as described in the last section, then the full swing should not cause you too many problems. If you can get the half swing correct, then all you have to do is extend it and you should be able to make a reasonable full swing.

Although I am still describing positions in the swing in this section, it is very difficult always to *feel* these positions in isolation throughout the swing. Perhaps the trained professional will be able to detect an imperfection at any stage during their swing, but you are unlikely to be that sensitive. By training with the help of the words and photographs in this book, ideally swinging where you can see yourself, perhaps with the aid of video, then you can learn a lot about your swing, and the mistakes you are most likely to make. Now grip the club at its full length and swing, at first in slow motion, trying to be aware of what you are doing. Then gradually increase the speed of the swing. Later I will give some ideas about how the swing should *feel*.

From the half-way position the arms continue to swing upwards, and the shoulders continue to turn, until they have turned at least 90° from the set-up. Now my wrists have fully cocked and there is a 90° angle between my left forearm and the shaft, which is virtually horizontal. My left arm has not remained totally straight, as this would create rigidity in the swing. Neither is it bent, but it is *slightly bowed*. My hips have turned about 45°, and my weight, which is now predominantly on the right side, is on the centre and inside of my right foot, with more towards the heel than at address. Most importantly, my right knee has retained its original flex. My left knee now points behind the ball, and my left heel has just eased off the ground. My head has rotated a little to the right, but has remained very steady. The swing has revolved around a central point which is the large bone at the top of my spine, which has remained centred.

This is where a good backswing is either maximized or completely wasted. The change of direction from swinging the club back to starting the downswing is perhaps the most crucial part of the swing. Even with the most perfect backswing, things can still go wrong. My *arms* start to swing down and my weight starts to move back to the left at the same time. My left arm is pulling down as my left knee and left hip move towards the target. This movement keeps the club on the inside, and importantly retains most of the angle between the left forearm and shaft. My left heel has returned to the ground. My head remains steady, and I am still focussing on the ball mainly with my left eye.

Just prior to impact, my arms have continued to swing *downwards*, and my wrists are uncocking, ready to deliver the clubhead at maximum speed into the back of the ball. My body has unwound in response to the swinging arms. My right knee is beginning to flex towards the ball. Notice that although most of my weight has been transferred to the left side, my head has remained behind the ball.

The full swing

Impact shows a marked similarity to the address position. The triangle of arms and shoulders is in evidence. The wrists have fully uncocked, the back of my left hand is very firm, and the hands are virtually as they were at address, still just ahead of the clubface. The left hip has started to open up (turn to the left), and the left foot is taking most of my weight. The right knee has kicked in so that it points ahead of the ball, and the right heel is just off the ground. Most importantly, the clubface is square, and still descending. My head and central hub have remained steady, and my eyes are now fixed to the back of the ball.

As my arms have continued to swing *through* the ball, my hands and arms have started to rotate slightly in an anti-clockwise direction. The momentum of my arms has turned my body through, so that the triangular pattern remains. My left hip still turns, creating space into which my arms can swing. As my right knee becomes more flexed, it is only the toes of that foot that remain on the ground.

The power of the right side is evident as my right arm straightens, and my right knee moves towards the left. My hands and arms have continued to rotate slightly anti-clockwise, and my wrists are beginning to cock upwards. My left elbow is folding so that it starts to point towards the ground. My head is also starting to rotate towards the target so as not to inhibit any power. Because of additional speed and power you will feel your right arm more extended at this point compared to a similar position in the half swing.

My arms and hands have swung the club upwards and over the left shoulder, and my body has turned through so that it faces to the left of the target. The completion of the swing shows good balance, with nearly all of the weight towards the outside and heel of the left foot, and the toes of the right foot providing extra support. My head has also rotated to face the target, which is an essential point to note.

The full swing

Again we pick the swing up from the half-way-back position. The photograph right illustrates beautifully how the clubface is still in a square position. By that I mean that from the half-way-back position, my wrists have continued to cock in the same sideways direction. At address the back of my forearm, left wrist and the leading edge of the clubface were in line, and they have remained in that relationship. Furthermore, my arms have swung on the correct plane, which places the leading edge of the clubhead about 45° to the horizon. My elbows have stayed a constant distance apart, with the right elbow now pointing downwards, and the spinal angle set at address has been retained. All these factors produce the correct plane to the swing. A simple plane guideline is to swing your left arm into the slot between your right shoulder and your head, but this does vary according to your height and the club used. The club shaft is parallel to the target line. Because of good posture, you can clearly see my right side turned out of the way, creating a space into which my arms have swung. Notice the flex of the right knee. The right leg is now absorbing a lot of pressure, since the majority of my weight is on that side. You can see and sense from the photograph above how the club has a direct and clear route back to the ball from the inside.

In the downswing the arms descend into the space created by the right side turning out of the way on the backswing. The right elbow is moving towards the ground. You can see that the club has remained on the inside track, and that there is no suggestion of the right shoulder being too powerful and throwing the club onto the outside path. The hips are starting to square up.

Just prior to impact you can sense that, as the wrists uncock, the right hand will provide much of the power. The right elbow is still bent. The left hip is just opening to the target line, and the right knee is starting to kick in. The club is approaching from the 3.30 direction, from the inside.

The full swing

At impact the upper body closely resembles the address position, with the shoulders virtually parallel to the target line, and the arms almost as they were. The left hip has opened a little more, and the right heel is off the ground. Most importantly, the clubface is square to the target.

This shows very nicely how the hands and arms have worked through the impact zone. The clubhead is starting to swing back to the inside, towards 8.00 o'clock, and quite correctly the clubface is starting to close to the target line. My hands and arms are rotating anti-clockwise. The spinal angle is still the same as at address.

The completion of the swing shows how fully the body has turned, and only now, once the ball is well on its way, my spine is a little more upright. Notice that my right side has released so that all the spikes on my right shoe are visible.

Address determines the shape of the swing

In the previous swing sequences I was using a 6 iron, and the shape of the swing was largely determined by my address position and length of the club. As these two factors alter, so will the shape and feel of your swing.

When using the middle irons, a 5, 6 or 7, the weight should be equally distributed on either foot, which will help you to produce a slightly downwards strike on the ball, and you should take a divot or at least some grass after impact.

The stance is progressively wider for the long irons, with the weight evenly distributed. Because the club shaft is longer, the attack on the ball is shallower, with only a small divot, or just the top layer of grass taken after impact.

For full shots with the 8, 9, wedge and sand wedge, as the stance narrows, the weight gradually starts to favour the left side. This, together with the shorter shaft, encourages a more descending strike, producing increased backspin, extra height, and control, and a larger divot.

The following pictures, where I am using a wedge, 6 iron and driver, show how the change of weight and ball position affect the swing. In the photographs taken from behind, you can see my posture change and length of club shaft have altered the plane of the swing. Shorter clubs are swung on a more upright plane, because you stand closer to the ball, while the driver is swung on a flatter plane because the longer shaft demands that you stand further from the ball. The exact plane will be determined by a person's height, which in turn affects the posture.

You may be a little weary of me emphasizing the importance of the set-up, but by now you can probably see why I have majored on this aspect.

The most important points to notice are ball ▶ position and weight distribution. Although the ball position for the wedge and 6 iron are the same, my weight is much more on the left side with the wedge, and equal with the 6 iron. With the driver, the ball is played further forward and the weight favours the right foot 60/40. Note how my head position alters.

Address determines the shape of the swing

The top-of-swing positions highlight the differences. Note how much less shoulder turn and weight transference is evident in the wedge compared to the driver. The swing with the shorter irons, such as an 8 or sand iron, will feel more arm-orientated, while the swing with longer clubs naturally develops more body turn and weight transference.

Address determines the shape of the swing

With the wedge (and other short irons) the posture and length of club dictate a more upright swing with less body turn. The same two factors influence the shape of the swing for the driver, but since my spine is more upright at address, and the shaft is longer, it encourages more turn, on a flatter plane. The plane of the 6 iron is between the wedge and driver. In each case my shoulders have turned at 90° to my spine. However, you should not think about these points as swing changes, they are pre-determined at address. The through swings with each club will vary slightly, according to their appropriate plane.

Swing faults and remedies

It is almost inevitable that there will be aspects of your swing that are rather less than perfect — nearly every golfer in the world has some imperfection in their action. In this section, I want to highlight some of the more common faults so that, if you spot a position that looks familiar, now is the time to change it before it becomes too ingrained. You may not be fully aware of how you swing, but your regular playing partners should be able to help you. However, by this stage, you have probably become aware of your swing deficiencies, and will be able to recognize some of the following horrors.

The right side has failed to clear on the backswing. The right hip is unable to turn due to bad posture with the seat tucked under at address, so the hips move laterally to the right, and the weight goes onto the outside of the right foot.

Remedy Correct the posture with the seat pushed to the rear, then be sure to turn the right side out of the way.

This swing has been made by moving the central hub of the body to the right, rather than keeping it steady. The left heel has released too much allowing this movement to take place. Instead of just pivoting around the central hub, this has become a combination of a pivot and sway.

Remedy Concentrate on pivoting opposite the ball without moving to the right. Keep the left heel much nearer, perhaps even on the ground for the more supple and slimmer players.

Swing faults and remedies

The arms have been swung too horizontally, and the right elbow is clamped to the side. This created a flat plane, caused by the clubhead going back too much on the inside, towards 5.00 o'clock.

Remedy Swing the clubhead back towards 3.00 o'clock for about 6 inches before letting it swing to the inside. Then have the feeling of swinging your arm *upwards,* so that your hand will feel more above your head.

The arms have been swung too upright and the right elbow no longer points to the ground. This would be called an upright plane, and can be caused by taking the club back in a straight line, towards 3.00 o'clock, for too long.

Remedy Try to keep your elbows the same width apart throughout the backswing, letting the clubhead come inside the target line towards 3.30 much sooner. Your hands will then feel much more behind rather than above your head at the top of the backswing.

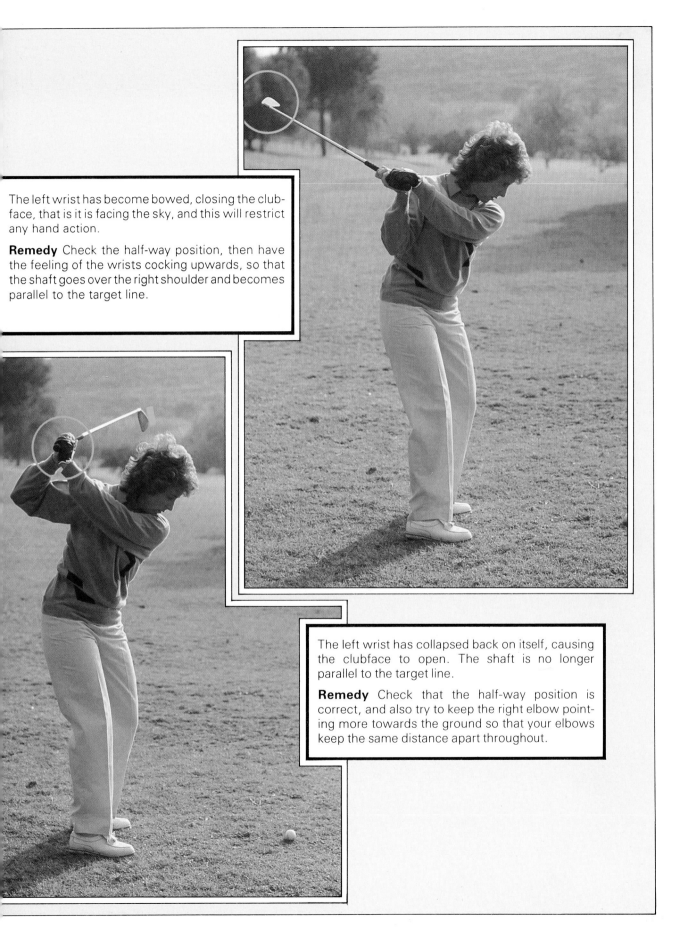

The left wrist has become bowed, closing the club-face, that is it is facing the sky, and this will restrict any hand action.

Remedy Check the half-way position, then have the feeling of the wrists cocking upwards, so that the shaft goes over the right shoulder and becomes parallel to the target line.

The left wrist has collapsed back on itself, causing the clubface to open. The shaft is no longer parallel to the target line.

Remedy Check that the half-way position is correct, and also try to keep the right elbow pointing more towards the ground so that your elbows keep the same distance apart throughout.

Swing faults and remedies

The left hand has become loose, and the club is therefore out of control. You should feel slightly increased pressure in these last three fingers at the top of the swing, and in this instance the hand has yielded to this strain.

Remedy Concentrate on maintaining grip pressure with the last three fingers throughout. Swinging with the left hand only helps you to appreciate just how much strain it has to withstand. If you let go at the top of the swing, it will become very obvious, and the club will probably fall to the ground.

The club has been swung back too far and is out of control. This is often due to the fault described left; taking the club back too fast; or the idea that a very long backswing will help to hit the ball a long way. It is better to have a shorter backswing that is in control.

Remedy Make what *feels* like a three-quarter or even half-length backswing, at a steady rather than fast pace. Try to stop your body turning and arms swinging at the same time, which should keep the shaft more parallel to the ground. You will then find it easier to use your hands at the correct time and strike the ball better and further.

Swing faults and remedies

The right leg has straightened and does not provide enough support at this stage. The legs will not work correctly in the downswing. The action will become just a heave with the top half of the body.

Remedy The leg has given way to the additional pressure it must take in the backswing. Practise swinging slowly at first but concentrating on keeping the original flex in the right knee.

This is called a reverse pivot. In the backswing the weight has moved onto the left side instead of the right. It is most likely to move to the right instead of the left in the downswing. It is often caused by being over-intent on keeping the head still.

Remedy During the backswing allow the weight to move very definitely onto the right side, so you will *feel* like you are swaying to the right. Do not worry about your head moving a little.

The right hip and shoulders have not turned enough and have caused the left elbow to collapse. It is bent not bowed. It will not be possible to pull down with the left arm from this position. Instead the hands will throw the club at the ball without sufficient arm swing.

Remedy Check the posture at address, as this may stop the hips turning, and also turn the right foot out a little. From the half-way position keep the hips and body turning, which will allow the left arm to stay straighter.

Swing faults and remedies

The spinal angle set at address has been lost, so that now the spine is almost upright, which causes the head to rise in the backswing. It will be impossible ever to make consistent contact with the ball (or any contact at all) from this position.

Remedy Concentrate on maintaining the angle set at address, and feel your left shoulder turn under your chin. At first it may make the swing feel cramped.

This is often caused by a reverse pivot (see page 61), which results in the weight being to the right at impact. Notice how the hands are level with the ball causing the club to hit the ground before the ball.

Remedy Be sure to transfer the weight to the right in the backswing, so that it has a chance to transfer back to the left side. Try to hit the ball into the ground, not up in the air.

Here the legs have moved the central hub too laterally towards the target, and there is too much weight on the left side. The hands are too far ahead of the clubhead and the ball will be topped.

Remedy Concentrate more on hand and arm action and less on leg drive, and try to keep your head behind the ball at impact.

Swing faults and remedies

This is the reverse-C position. The spine is curved backwards, which can be painful and harmful, and is no use to the swing. It is often caused by trying to keep the head down for too long into the follow through.

Remedy After the ball is struck allow the head to rotate towards the target, and let the weight go almost fully onto the left foot and towards the heel. Your body will then face the target, and your head must finish more above the left foot, with the spine straighter (see page 43).

These are some simple remedies for common faults, but I would recommend you to refer back to pages 34-53 and re-read the relevant parts, comparing these photographs with the equivalent ones in that section.

Chapter 2

Perfecting your long game

Once you have learnt the basic principles of swinging the club correctly, refining that movement to produce satisfying shots is the next task. This chapter explains in some detail how your swing should feel, and gives a few swing thoughts that may help you produce good rhythm and timing, which for ladies is essential. Hitting the ball far enough can be a problem, so the sections on fairway woods and driving should be invaluable in this respect.

Part of the fun of golf is trying to manoeuvre the ball which, once you have overcome the initial learning stages of the game, is really not as difficult as it may seem. Sloping lies and awkward stances can present a problem if you do not know how to cope with them. This chapter will help you to sort these out, and explains the right way to tackle shots from the rough, which so often ruin a good score.

Even the best golfers develop faults, so I have analyzed why the bad shots occur and how to cure them. This will help you to improve your handicap, and your enjoyment of the game.

Applying your swing correctly to the many different shots that are required during a round is something that the beginner may find rather daunting. By continually referring back to this chapter, soon you will be able readily to change your set-up and swing for every occasion.

Swing concepts

The full swing and half swing sections (pages 34-47) have illustrated in great detail the physical movements and clubhead positions that are desirable in the swing. Even though the strike may not be perfect yet, if the shape of the swing is beginning to look correct, then you have made a solid start, and good contact will come with practice.

If you are very new to the game, please be patient with yourself because, as I'm sure you have discovered by now, you have chosen one of the most exacting sports in existence. Methodically build your swing, so that little by little conscious movements become subconscious. Anyone who has learnt to drive a car must have felt on the first few lessons that they would never manage to give a hand signal, look in the mirror, change gear, steer and miss other cars all at once. You have to keep repeating new movements to create muscle memory, so eventually you cope with more actions subconsciously, whether they involve driving a car or hitting a golf ball. In each case, practice makes the learning process faster, so try to swing the golf club, or work on your new grip and set-up as often as possible.

Having shown you how the swing should look, here are some ideas on how the swing should feel. Feel is very subjective, and two people performing the same actions are likely to describe what they feel they are doing in two different ways. However, you may benefit from the following ideas and thoughts. You have had a visual input on the swing, now is the time for some mental impressions.

● As you stand at address, imagine that you are going to swing the clubhead in a circle around fixed point,that of the large bone at the top of your spine.

● Feel that the club is swung back smoothly. If you rush it, the whole swing will tend to be jerky. Try to synchronize the arm swing and body turn.

● As the backswing progresses, you should feel additional pressure on your right leg and in the last three fingers of your left hand. The underneath of the upper part of your left arm (the triceps area) will feel stretched, as will the left side of your body.

● Do not be obsessed with keeping your head perfectly still. A *little* sideways movement is acceptable for the beginner until greater suppleness allows you to make a good turn. Keeping your head still stifles a good shoulder turn. More importantly, try not to let your head move up and down. If this happens it is because the spinal angle set at address has altered. This angle should stay the same until well into the follow through.

● You should have the feeling, especially with the driver, of coiling behind the ball, with a sense of tautness in the left side, and this tautness must be retained as the downswing commences.

● The change of direction is perhaps the most crucial part of the swing, *do not rush it*. The downward arm swing and movement of weight back towards the left side, must be unified, smooth and unhurried. Problems arise when players just cannot wait to 'have a go' at the ball, and throw the clubhead towards the ball on the wrong path in an uncontrolled manner. Any tautness that existed at the top of the swing is immediately lost. Alternatively some golfers leap over onto their left leg, overdoing the weight transference.

I like to use the roller coaster as an analogy. As it climbs to the top of the slope it seems to come almost to a halt. It moves steadily over the summit, and gradually accelerates as it descends until, by the bottom of the slope, it is at maximum speed. The golf swing is very similar, because you want maximum clubhead speed at the base of the arc (bottom of the slope) to coincide with impact. So change direction by swinging your arms and gently moving your left knee towards the target, reserving any hand action until it is needed nearer the impact zone.

Swing concepts

● For the more experienced golfer, once the downswing has commenced, much of what follows is pure natural reaction. The swinging weight of the clubhead, due to the outward, or centrifugal, force in the swing, tends to uncock the wrists, and the feeling is one of the clubhead free-wheeling through the ball. However, for the beginner this feeling is so often far from natural. There is a tendency to over-control the club, tighten the grip, and deny the swing the power that may have been derived from good hand and wrist action. The wrists are a swinging hinge, and it is just at impact that they fully recover their original position, which guarantees power and accuracy. So after you have started the downswing with your arms and have transferred a little weight as the clubhead is approaching the impact zone, use your hands and feel that you throw the clubhead past the ball.

● Many of my pupils respond well to the idea that the right hand and right knee move through impact together, with the right hand and arm starting to turn over the left. Anyone who has played tennis should feel that it is like hitting a top-spin forehand to the left court, where the right hand rotates anti-clockwise.

● The original concept was one of swinging the clubhead in a circle. Try not to become what is called 'ball bound'. Do not allow your attention to focus on hitting at the ball, but on swinging the clubhead *through* the impact zone, into a well-balanced finish, facing the target. As I have said, the golf swing is not a series of positions, but a continuous flowing movement. If you are capable of making a good backswing, and have the correct action through the impact zone, then from the top of the backswing your thoughts should be to attain that balanced finish. For the beginner, who may be struggling to get their legs and arms working in unison, I would recommend practising without the ball, concentrating on swinging to the finish position. If you can do that, then your legs will be more likely to work automatically, and you will start to swing *through*, and not *at* the ball. The feeling of throwing the clubhead over your left shoulder should help you to swing through as well.

Even a top professional's swing does not necessarily feel the same from day to day. When top players warm up prior to their round, they are not just stretching their muscles, they are also finding out which swing thought or feeling is going to produce the perfect shot. It may well be a totally different thought or feeling to the one that worked the previous day or week. Methodically work through these examples on feel, and see if some ideas give you better results than others. You will not be able to incorporate more than one idea at a time, although it is possible to have one to help with your set-up, and another for your swing. Give each of my ideas a fair trial, but also try to develop some of your own. These particular

feel-thoughts are those to which I can relate, you may respond better to some of your own.

Timing

You have probably realised by now that golf necessitates using all the body's muscles. However, muscles do not all work most efficiently at the same pace. So there has to be a compromise, where the faster muscles, such as those in the hands and arms, work only at a pace that accommodates the larger muscles, such as those in the back and thighs. Beginners sometimes think that the ball can be hit further by swinging their arms faster, but this reduces the contribution that the back and shoulders can make, and the swing is denied power and direction. Similarly, if the downswing is rushed, the thigh muscles do not have time to work, and the tautness experienced at the top of the swing is dissipated. Some golfers try to copy top professionals who accentuate their leg action but, because they do not possess the same strength of hand action as the professional, the outcome is usually a thin or cut shot. Correct timing of the golf swing calls for a balance of pace between muscles, which takes time and practice to achieve. Beginners need to concentrate on making what seem to be very mechanical movements, and until such time as they acquire a little more fluency they must just accept that they will hit their share of poor shots.

For the more experienced player, who perhaps feels that she swings the club quite well but without due reward, here are two simple guides to analyzing and correcting timing.

If your shots tend to fade and slice, or you thin quite a few, then your leg action is too strong for your hand and arm action. You must concentrate on a stronger arm swing, practising hitting balls with your feet together until the strike improves.

If your shots draw or hook, and you hit a lot of fat shots, then your leg action is not lively enough. You should put more emphasis on pulling with your left arm, and moving your left knee more emphatically from the top of the swing. With your arms hanging in front of you, take a club and hold either end of the shaft horizontally with your arms shoulder-width apart. Now make a swing, and you should find that your legs work more fluently.

Remember that you swing the golf club about 20 feet in an arc before you strike the ball. If you are half an inch or one degree out, you have hit a less than perfect shot. As your strength increases so the timing of your swing may alter slightly, so don't be too hard on yourself. By paying a little more attention to the timing of your swing, you may get closer to that perfect strike.

Tempo

Timing and tempo are very much inter-related in the swing. Timing is the sequence in which different parts of the body move. Tempo is the pace at which all this movement takes place, and

Swing concepts

has a direct bearing on the timing of the swing. So, what is the correct tempo for you, and how do you find it? It has been said that your tempo reflects your character, that a person who is always dashing about will swing the club quickly, and vice versa. To some extent this may be true, but the overriding factor, whatever your character, is clubhead control.

It is self-defeating to swing the clubhead faster than you can control it, no matter whether you are by nature the tortoise or the hare. But what you are trying to achieve is a golf *swing*, and to that end there must be a certain degree of pace, or else all sense of rhythm is lost.

The pace of the backswing will have a direct affect on the pace of the downswing and, as already mentioned, this is likely to change as your swing and strength develop. I have to advise many more male players to slow down their swing than I have to ask to speed it up. With the extra strength men possess in their hands and arms, they are often guilty of making short, quick backswings without turning their shoulders.

This is naturally not such a common error in women, but for them a quick backswing will result often in a long backswing, where control is lost. On the other hand, I have found women players who I believe swing the club too slowly. They seem to *take* the club back instead of swinging it back. They fail to create any rhythm in the swing, which leads to a very uncoordinated downswing, and usually lack leg action.

The backswing not only positions the club, it serves to create the pace and rhythm. Golf teachers spend a lot of time trying to get a pupil into a good position at the top of the swing. You might ask, if this position is so important, why don't we start from this point? Well, we don't because a good backswing helps to create good rhythm and tempo.

How to find your best tempo

Take a 6 iron and hit some shots from good lies at your normal pace, noting distance and accuracy. Now hit a similar amount of shots with first of all a faster and then a slower tempo, and again note where the balls land. From this you may be surprised to find that, by swinging at what feels to be three-quarters of your normal pace, you have hit the balls further and straighter. On the other hand, a slightly faster tempo may reveal that your control of the clubhead is now good enough for you to put a little more speed into the swing. Of course, you may already swing at your optimum tempo. Whatever the outcome it is always an interesting exercise to return to from time to time.

You may also benefit from making a few swings without the club, by just interlocking your two hands. You will find it easier to make a smoother unhurried swing without the club or ball to distract you.

Here is one last example of good timing and tempo, to which I'm sure many of you can relate. Imagine a shot from the fairway that has to carry a hazard and for which you need a good 3 wood. To be safe you decide to lay up short of the hazard, so you select a 6 iron, and make a smooth, unhurried swing. To your surprise, the ball zooms off into the distance and lands in or very near the hazard, and you wish you had been more courageous and hit the 3 wood. This has happened because during the swing you relaxed and made what felt like a three-quarter-paced and -length swing. In fact you achieved perfect timing and tempo. Had you used the 3 wood, you might have tried to thrash the ball, resulting in poor timing and tempo and a bad shot.

Keep this example in your mind when you play and see if, with improved timing and tempo, the mechanics in your swing take a turn for the better. Top class golfers are always searching for good rhythm. Even for them it is something that can be perfect one day and gone the next, so don't worry if this happens to you, just keep perservering.

This is one of the most important sections of this book. What women lack in strength, they can compensate for with good timing and tempo. I have played many pro-ams with men who are usually quite surprised just how far I can hit the ball, with seemingly little effort. I would expect to hit a 5 iron shot about 155 yards (I am 5 feet 3 inches tall, and weigh about 125 pounds). I enhance my sound technique by concentrating on maintaining good timing and tempo, which result in maximum clubhead speed at impact.

Long irons versus fairway woods

Even a raw beginner wants to hit the ball a long way from the fairway, and one of the clubs designed for this purpose is a long iron. Bearing this in mind, many lady golfers shun their woods completely, feeling that they are to be used only once they have mastered their irons. Such thinking really only serves to make the game more difficult, for the fairway woods, which they still take out with them on the course, could be their salvation.

The long irons are difficult to use, for the following reasons:

1. The 2, 3 and 4 irons do not have very much loft on them, and so any unwanted sidespin is accentuated.

2. The small head on the iron does not exactly inspire confidence, which as we all know is one of the most important assets in golf.

3. The long shafts in these irons tend to make them more unwieldy, and consequently the player is likely to lose some control.

The outcome is that when a long iron is needed, the beginner swings erratically in an effort to hit the ball harder, usually trying to scoop the ball into the air, for fear that insufficient loft on the club will not get the ball airborne. The ball is frequently topped or hit thinly, and will only scuttle along the ground a short distance.

It would be fair to say that with a long iron, a certain degree of strength in the hands and wrists is needed to produce the clubhead speed that will promote the amount of backspin required to hit the ball a decent distance through the air.

Often the average lady golfer, especially the beginner, does not possess this strength, and may well struggle in vain to produce crisp long iron shots until she has been playing long enough to have developed both the speed of hand and quality of technique required. It is only when the ball is teed up that she may be able to 'get away with' her deficiency, but of course this is of no use on the fairways.

The correct swing for the long irons is no different from that for the middle irons, but the control is a little more demanding. For the more experienced player, one way to improve is to hit perhaps twenty 6 irons, then hit five to ten 3 irons, concentrating on keeping the same rhythm and action. Use a low tee, or sit the ball on a cushion of grass, and keep alternating clubs.

The beginner and higher handicap player need not despair, because in recent years both the professional player and the manufacturer have come to your rescue. Whilst many years ago it was considered a last resort to use very lofted fairway woods, in our enlightened times even world-class professionals, both men and women, are using their 5, 6 and 7 woods, roughly equivalent to the 2, 3 and 4 irons, to great effect. So why should it be easier to hit these clubs well?

1. They have more loft than the equivalent iron, and so unwanted sidespin is reduced, resulting in straighter shots.

2. The appearance of the club with its chubby head somehow makes the golfer feel that she has a club in her hands that will hit the ball a long way. There is a solid look to it, compared to the small, insignificant blade of a long iron.

3. The fairway wood is best struck at the base of the arc, sweeping the ball from the grass en route. This strike characteristic lends itself quite well to the action of many lady golfers, who often experience trouble hitting down on the ball, especially with the longer irons.

These three important factors will increase the player's confidence, and certainly improve their chance of producing a sound rhythmical swing, resulting in a good strike.

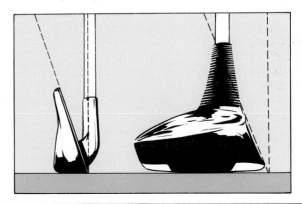

Long irons v. fairway woods

This set-up should dictate that the swing has good width. My head is nicely behind the ball, which is positioned about 2-3 inches inside the left heel. From here, visualize sweeping the ball from the turf, just taking the top layer of grass rather than a divot.

This swing sequence reveals the benefit of the ▶ correct set-up. The clubhead remains close to the ground at the start of the backswing, as a result of a coordinated movement of the body and arms. The clubhead approaches the ball from a shallow inside path and then sweeps the ball from the turf. The balanced finish is due to good leg work and the ambition to swing *through,* rather than *at* the ball.

If you do not play your fairway woods very well, first check your address position, then keep the clubhead low to the ground until it passes your right foot. Be certain to give yourself time to make a good body turn in the backswing, then think of swinging *through,* sweeping the ball from the turf.

Long irons versus fairway woods

Fairway woods from bad lies
If the ball is in a bad lie or in light rough, and you need distance, then your fairway woods are your salvation. You will be able to gain good distance, providing the lie is not extremely bad, and will find that from the rough, the club will glide through the grass better than even a medium iron. Long grass tends to tangle around the hosel of the iron, closing the blade, which makes a good shot rather difficult, but this does not happen with the wood. Depending on how bad the lie may be, you can use a 4, 5, 6 or 7 wood quite satisfactorily, but do not wade into deep rough with a 3 wood in your hands, as even a top-class player would not do that.

The swing should be made primarily by swinging the arms *up* in the backswing, with less emphasis than usual on shoulder turn. You may not be able to swing through as fully, since the clubhead will meet more resistance at impact.

Summary
Having read this section, I hope that players who have so far neglected the fairway woods, will endeavour to use them more often. Given a reasonable technique, you should be pleasantly surprised at how much distance you can gain from them with relatively little effort. The more you use them, the better you will become acquainted with their versatility, and who knows, perhaps they might be promoted to your favourite clubs in the bag.

The main alteration to make is at address. Move the ball back towards the centre of your stance, but keep your hands ahead of the clubface and place a little more weight on your left side. This will encourage you to strike the ball while the clubhead is still descending (rather than at the base of the arc) — vital as the ball is sitting in a hollow. The address adjustments mean that the back edge of the club will be off the ground, and you will have de-lofted the club a touch. Also stand a little closer to the ball, and choke down (slide your hands down) slightly on the grip. These changes will help you to make a more upright swing, thus enabling you to strike down on the ball.

Driving ... how to split the fairway

Many women players experience difficulty in getting adequate distance from the tee. The driver is the most unforgiving club in your bag, despite the fact that its large head may make it look the most likely for giving the ball a hearty thump. So why is it such a difficult club to use?

The less loft on a club, the more likely it is to impart sidespin, the spin that moves the ball from left to right or vice versa. This is because the ball is contacted near its equator, creating greater sidespin than backspin. The exact opposite is true when using clubs at the other end of the set, such as the wedge, where backspin will override side-spin, making it more difficult to hit the ball so that it curves.

The driver has the least loft in the set, varying between 7-13° and this highlights imperfections. Unfortunately, some of the drivers in ladies' sets are not very 'kind' clubs: they have insufficient loft,

which means that all but the lower-handicap golfers would be better not using them. So first get the loft on your driver checked. If it is less than 10°, and is not a metal wood, I suggest you sell it or put it out of harm's way, because it is going to cause you problems. If it has 11-13°, and your handicap is less than 18, the club is probably suitable, or you could drop back to your 3 wood, which has more loft. If you are a beginner, or your handicap is more than 18, you would be better off driving with the 3 wood in your set. You will sacrifice a little distance, but you will more than compensate for this by increased accuracy.

Before I describe how to hit a driver, I'd like to give you one or two tips on teeing the ball. This is the one time you can choose where to play the ball from, so take full advantage. Select an area that is flat and even both for the club's path, and for your feet. Try to avoid wet muddy areas, or depressions in the tee, even if this means teeing up behind the markers. Remember, you have an area up to two club lengths back from the markers, and making the hole 1-2 yards longer is worth it for a good foothold.

Always tee up on the same side as any trouble. If there is out-of-bounds or a hazard on the left, tee up on the left side, and then you will be hitting away from the trouble.

The height you tee the ball is important. Correctly teed, the top half of the ball should be above the top of the clubhead at address. If you tee the ball too high, the club may go almost completely under it; if too low, this tends to promote a downward strike — not what you want!

Driving

The secret of getting maximum distance with the driver is good clubhead speed, plus a shallow inside attack. When using the driver, you may find it helpful to have your shoulders *slightly* closed — aimed a touch more to the right than normal, as this will encourage an inside path. Also, it will prevent you from falling into a common error created by the ball position. The ball is played from the most forward point with the driver, and this makes it very easy for your shoulders to be pulled open and aimed left, which will cause a steep out-to-in attack on the ball, just what you want to avoid. So if you consciously close them a little to start with, making sure your right shoulder feels much lower than your left, this should help to guarantee the correct angle of attack. At address visualize the swing path of the clubhead: back and down on a path at about 3.30.

Your head must be behind the ball, which is just inside your left heel. Your weight must favour the right side 60/40, to encourage the slightly ascending strike required. To facilitate a full turn, angle out your right foot a little more, and rotate your head slightly to the right, so that you have the feeling of focusing on the back of the ball with your left eye.

The set-up helps to ensure that the clubhead swings away low and wide, with no suggestion of the hands picking it up. The width in the back-swing is provided by the arms and body swinging in unison; there is no need to *stretch* your arms away from your body.

At the top of the swing there is a sense of coiling behind the ball, with most of the weight now on the right leg. Depending on your suppleness, you can raise your left heel accord-

ingly, but only towards the end of the backswing. Don't worry if your head moves a *little* laterally to the right, as it is essential that you have a good weight transference to the right. Don't be misled by the 'I must keep my head still' adage: many top professionals allow a little head movement to develop with the longer clubs. Keep your head and central hub as *steady* as you can. Note that although my head has moved behind the ball at the top of the swing, the central hub — the top of

my spine — has remained virtually as it was at address. Compare this to the bad position on page 61 (top), which is the result of keeping the head well and truly anchored. The clubface is square, facing between vertical and horizontal.

The impact position shows how my head has remained behind the ball, as my arms continue to swing. I have the feeling of the clubhead free-wheeling away from me, towards 9.30, as it accelerates through the ball.

Driving

1 Attacking the ball from the inside is one of the most important aspects of long driving. Here you can see quite clearly that from the top the club is swung down on the inside.

Once the ball has been struck, the weight continues to move onto the left leg as the whole of the left side turns out of the way. The finish position is a result of the sheer momentum of the swing, with the body turning so much it faces left of target, and most of the weight on the outside of the left foot, with the right heel fully released from the ground. The head moves towards the target a little, so that the spine is almost vertical at this point. To hit the ball a long way, you must endeavour to swing to a full, well balanced finish.

2 During the backswing the right side of the body has turned out of the way, and it is into this space that the arms swing. If the right shoulder had been used, instead of the left arm pulling down the clubhead, it would have thrown the club onto an outside track.

3 You must be able to visualize the swing path of the club through the impact zone. Ideally this should be towards 9.30, as you allow the right hand and arm start to rotate over the left, giving a gently curving draw that produces more distance. In the picture you can see that the clubface is closing from the target line soon after impact.

Do not be tempted to thrash the driver, as you will probably make poor contact. Concentrate on maintaining the same rhythm you would use for the 6 iron, then you will strike the ball better, and it will go further.

Perhaps one of the most common faults is skying the drive, where the ball goes very high and not very far. This happens because the clubhead approaches the ball too steeply, often due to a bad set-up, with the weight either too equally distributed or favouring the left side. Once the set-up is correct, always keep the clubhead low to the ground, at least until it has passed your right foot, as this helps to create a good turn. Keep your head behind the ball through impact, and don't be in a hurry to transfer the weight completely onto the left side until the ball has been struck.

If you use a 3 wood, once you start to hit the fairway consistently, then progress to a driver, but please consult a professional before buying one, as your choice can make a lot of difference to your game.

Manoeuvring the ball

There will be situations on the course when you will want to shape a shot, to curve the ball either right or left, or hit it high or low. Whilst the complete beginner may believe this is beyond her capabilities, you may be pleasantly surprised to find these shots not really that difficult. Any golf shot requires clubhead control, and once you have mastered the initial difficulties of the game, and can swing the club in a *freely* controlled manner, there is no reason why you should not attempt to manoeuvre the ball, especially if the alternative shots are not very appealing.

The intentional fade

Aim the clubface at the target and with the ball further forward in your stance set your feet and shoulders open and aiming parallel to the initial direction in which you intend the ball to travel. Your hands will naturally be in a weaker position on the grip. This set-up will automatically create an out-to-in swing path — more in the 2.00-8.00 o'clock direction, but the clubface will be open, which will give the ball left-to-right spin. These alterations alone should create a soft fade without your making any conscious swing changes. Pick a spot a few feet in front of the ball over which you want it to start, then concentrate on sending it in that direction. By increasing the degree you aim your body to the left you will increase the curve to the right until the fade becomes a slice. If these changes alone do not produce sufficient curve, experiment with the following tips:

1 Think about swinging your arms slightly more upright, rather than creating a big shoulder turn.

2 Keep your left-hand grip firmer than usual, and your left hand and arm in control and ahead of the clubface. This will inhibit forearm rotation through impact and you will be able to maintain the open clubface position.

The player who naturally draws the ball may need to emphasize some of these actions.

The intentional draw

Aim the clubface at the target, and with the ball further back in your stance aim your feet and shoulders right of the target, parallel to the initial direction in which you want the ball to travel.

Your hands will naturally be in a stronger position than usual on the grip, and the grip pressure should be lighter. This set-up will automatically create an in-to-out swing path, more in the 4.00-10.00 o'clock direction, but the clubface will be closed, which will spin the ball right-to-left. These set-up alterations alone should produce a soft draw, without your making any conscious swing changes; just concentrate on starting the ball over an intermediate target just ahead of it. By increasing the degree you aim to the right of the target, the right-to-left draw shape will become stronger, developing into a hook.

If these changes alone do not produce the desired effect, try experimenting with these tips:
1 Make a good shoulder turn, and feel your arms swing a little flatter than usual.

2 Allow your right hand to rotate over the left through impact.

Players who slice may need to emphasize some of these actions.

These are the correct principles for intentional fading and drawing, but your own swing characteristics will mean that you will be able to bend the ball more readily one way than the other. Spend some time on the practice ground experimenting before being too ambitious on the course. Each player needs to know just how much to emphasize certain movements in order to shape the shot as desired.

Here are a few points worth remembering before you play either shot:
1 It is easier to fade the straighter-faced clubs.

2 It is harder to control the draw with the straighter-faced clubs.

3 A faded shot flies higher, loses distance, and does not roll much on landing.

4 A drawn shot flies lower, gains distance, and rolls more on landing.

5 It is easier to fade than draw from bad lies.

6 It is harder to shape the ball either way if a lot of grass intervenes between clubface and ball.

Manoeuvring the ball

Hitting high shots

Obviously the lofted irons hit the ball high, but you may need both distance and height on a shot, perhaps to carry a tree. Set up with the ball further forward in your stance, your weight a little more on the right foot, with the right knee flexed more inwards than usual. This sets your right shoulder much lower than the left, and positions your head more behind the ball. Your hands will be about level with the ball, rather than ahead of it, and the clubface will be laid back (but remains square to the target), so there is additional effective loft on the club. Swing your arms a fraction higher in the backswing, with a little more wrist action, then through impact try to keep your weight a bit more on your right side than usual, feeling the right hand working under rather than over the left. You do need a good lie for this shot; to hit a high shot from a bad lie, hit an intentional fade.

Hitting low shots

Naturally, the long irons hit the ball lower, but you may wish to play lower shots (perhaps into the wind) with other clubs. Play the ball well back in your stance, keeping your hands and head in front of it, your weight favouring the left side, and choke down on the grip a little. This set-up hoods the clubface (but it remains square to the target), reducing effective loft from the club. You should now find it easy to create a wide, firmer wristed swing that punches the ball forwards. The finish is curtailed, with the hands, arms and club pointing more towards the target, and not over your left shoulder.

Compare the last two address positions, and you can see how I have adapted my set-up, which dictates how I swing the club.

Manoeuvring the ball

Uneven lies

It is only on the tee that you can be assured of a level stance and a good lie, so it is important to know how to play shots from uneven parts of the course, and from less than perfect lies. So often in golf, if you know how the ball is likely to react, then you can allow for it, and the result can be quite satisfying. But if you don't know how to tackle a severe downhill lie for instance, then you'll end up frittering shots away.

Uphill lie During the swing, the clubhead should follow the contour of the slope as much as possible, so there is almost a feeling of hitting up through impact. It is difficult to use your legs as well as usual, therefore the hands are likely to become more active, closing the clubhead through impact. The ball will probably finish to the left of where you aim, so allow for this by aiming right of your target.

Uphill lie

With an uphill lie from the fairway, you need to set your spine at right angles to the slope, just as it would be at right angles to the ground on a level surface. This means putting extra weight on your right foot, with your right shoulder lower than usual. This set-up will add effective loft to your club; depending on the severity of the slope, a 5 iron could have the loft of a 6 or 7, so you need to use a less lofted club. Position the ball a little nearer your left foot, which will help to sweep the ball away.

Uphill lie When playing uphill shots around the green, you should lean into the slope, with more weight on your left leg, so that your spine is more at right angles to the horizontal. This will encourage you to hit into the slope causing the clubhead to come to an abrupt halt. On gentle slopes the better player may be able to play this shot leaning away from the slope, producing a higher softer shot.

Downhill lie

For a downhill lie you have to set your spine at right angles to the slope of the ground by putting more weight on your left leg, with your left shoulder very much lower than usual, and the ball well back in your stance. This set-up will deduct effective loft from the club so, depending on the severity of the slope, a 5 iron could have the loft of a 3 or 4. You should therefore select a club with more loft.

Downhill lie You can also use this set-up for many shots around the green, but where the slope is severe you will have to play the shot differently. To maintain your balance set your spine at right angles to the horizontal, but still play the ball back in your stance. In extreme circumstances you may find yourself playing the ball outside the right foot, and gripping the club right down on the shaft.

● To help you get the correct adjustments for fairway shots from uphill and downhill lies, remember it this way: weight to the low foot, and ball to the high. If you have trouble remembering that, low and weight both have a 'W'.

Downhill lie The swing is made primarily with the hands and arms, with little body turn or weight transference. You must swing the clubhead along the contour of the slope, which, if the ground rises steeply behind the ball, means swinging your arms up with an early wrist break. It is essential that you then swing the clubhead down the slope, resisting all temptation to try to help the ball into the air. Keep the right knee moving towards the target. The ball is likely to fade or be pushed to the right, so allow for this when you take aim.

Manoeuvring the ball

Sidehill lie . . . ball above the feet

Up- and downhill lies require altered weight distribution, but for sidehill shots you will need to change your posture.

When the ball is above your feet, you do not need to bend forward so much from the hips. So keeping your spine more upright, more weight towards your heels, choke down a little on the club, and position the ball more centrally in your stance. This set-up will cause you to swing on a flatter plane, resulting in a drawn shot, so aim to the right to allow for it. If the lie is not too severe, you can easily play a fairway wood when you need distance.

For shots around the green, make similar adjustments, allowing for the shot to pull to the left.

Sidehill lie . . . ball below the feet

Playing the ball from below your feet is one of the most disliked shots in the game. Keeping your balance is the key, once you have made the set-up adjustments. The ball is lower than normal, so stand a little closer, bend more from the hips, increase your knee flex, and be sure to grip at the end of the club. You will have more weight towards your toes than usual, but keep sufficient on your heels to maintain balance.

This set-up results in an upright three-quarter hand and arm swing only with little body turn, which creates an out-to-in swing path. This causes the ball to fade, and thus lose distance, so you should take a less lofted club than normal, and aim left of target. However, on severe slopes, especially where distance is needed, it would be unwise to take a very straight-faced club; instead be content with keeping the ball in play. As a rough guide, higher handicap ladies and beginners would be better using nothing more than a 5 iron. Try to stay down through the shot, and feel that you punch the ball away with your hands and arms. Do *not* try to hit the ball hard. The main danger with this shot is falling forwards and shanking the ball, so it is crucial to remain balanced.

Similar adjustments are needed for shots around the green, aiming left to allow for the ball drifting to the right.

With all shots from hilly lies, keeping your balance is one of the main keys, so always have a practice swing to test the feel of the shot as well

as to check your balance. More often than not a three-quarter swing will prove successful, although occasionally from a gentle sidehill lie with the ball above your feet, you can swing more aggressively.

Manoeuvring the ball

Playing from the rough

It has to be admitted that strength is involved in hitting from the rough, but you can get round this to a great extent if you know how to play the shot correctly. I think your first criterion must be to get the ball back onto the fairway in one shot, even if that means taking a more lofted club; in other words, don't be greedy by trying to make up for your mistakes. So often I see players wading into quite deep rough with a 3 wood, simply because there is still a long way to the hole. This is bad planning, since they are likely to take two or three shots to get back to the fairway. There are two methods of playing from the rough, depending on the situation.

Choice of club

Choice of club is governed by the lie, and the situation. Obviously from light rough the shot is not too difficult, although distance and accuracy may be impaired.
- If you wish to play a shot that comes out low and runs, choose method 1.
- If you wish to play a higher shot that does not run too much, choose method 2.
- Clubs to avoid are the long irons; instead if you need distance, use a high-numbered wood, perhaps choking down on it for extra control.
- In rough that is about 2 inches deep, where the whole of the ball is below the top of the grass, use a short iron.
- In deeper rough use the sand iron and be content at getting back onto the fairway. The extra weight in this club will help you to cut through the rough.

The very good lie in the rough

You may be lucky enough to find your ball sitting up in the rough, on top of the grass, almost as though it were on a tee. The one problem to recognize is that the clubhead could go completely under the ball, in which case contact is made only with the top edge of the club, and the result is poor. To overcome this, at address keep the clubhead level with the ball, and do not nestle it into the grass as you could dislodge it and incur a penalty. Your set-up should be the same as for a fairway shot, but you could put a little more weight on the right foot for exceptionally good lies. Swing the club a little flatter than normal, sweeping the ball off the grass. If the lie is very good, you could use a 3 or 4 wood and cash in on your luck!

Method 1 Position the ball well back in your stance. Place more weight on your left leg, and keep your hands ahead of the ball, so that the shaft slopes towards the target. The reason for setting-up in this manner is to encourage a steep angle of attack. Because there is a lot of grass behind the ball, you need to swing the club up steeply, or else it will get caught up. Likewise on the downswing, if the clubhead approaches from its normal path, too much grass will intervene between it and the ball. So from your set-up think mainly of swinging the clubhead up steeply away from the ball, then hit down as hard as you can. The set-up reduces the effective loft on the club, and because the intervening grass prevents backspin, the ball will come out lower than usual and run on landing. One more tip: grip more firmly to offset the extra resistance of the grass.

Method 2 Position the ball centrally in your stance, but open the clubface and aim your feet and shoulders just slightly left of the target. This set-up will promote a steep out-to-in swing path, with an open clubface. The club will not impart much sidespin because of the intervening grass, but the ball should come out quite high on a line between swing path and clubface. Again grip firmly and try to keep the left hand in control throughout.

Playing out of divots

When the ball lies in a divot you have to make a more upright swing than normal. If the clubhead approaches from its usual angle, you will not make contact with the bottom of the ball, and the shot will be topped or thinned. Play the shot as described in method 1, in this chapter, punching down firmly into the back of the ball, with little follow through. Because of the set-up, the club will have less effective loft, so the ball will fly lower than usual. If the ball is sitting at the back of the divot it is almost impossible to get a lot of height on it, so consider this when planning the shot. If the ball is sitting at the front of the divot, you should be able to hit it a little higher, but the direction may be affected if it is deflected by the edge of the divot. Middle and short irons, *not* long irons, are best for these shots, but the stronger player may find a lofted fairway wood is good from a shallow divot, when length is needed.

Slices, hooks and other imperfect shots

When you think that a perfect shot requires the clubhead to be swung about 20 feet in a given circle through the air before the ball is struck, the exacting nature of the sport becomes awesomely clear. If you are a quarter of an inch or one degree out, you have hit a less than perfect shot. But don't be daunted, you can play extremely respectable and enjoyable golf as long as you learn how to keep the degree of imperfection in check. Fairways are not so narrow, nor greens so small, that only a perfectly hit shot will find them: on every golf course there is a margin for error.

For the beginner, making contact with the bottom of the ball (getting the correct depth of strike by completing the radius at impact) is usually the first hurdle. If this is achieved, even though the clubface may be slightly open or closed, the ball gets airborne, even though it may veer right or left. The next stage is to get the ball airborne *and*

reasonably straight, and this is what all golfers seek to achieve for as long as they play the game. So don't despair if your shots are too banana-shaped for your liking, even Nancy Lopez, Laura Davies and Seve Ballesteros hit shots like this from time to time.

To help correct your faults, here is a simple analysis of why (in clubhead terms) they occur. The three main factors that govern the ball's flight are:
1 the direction in which the clubhead is swinging, called the swing path;
2 the direction in which the clubface is aimed;
3 the angle of attack.
Generally speaking, the ball will start its journey in the direction the clubhead is swung, then curve in the direction of the clubface. So let's refer back to the clock face analogy.

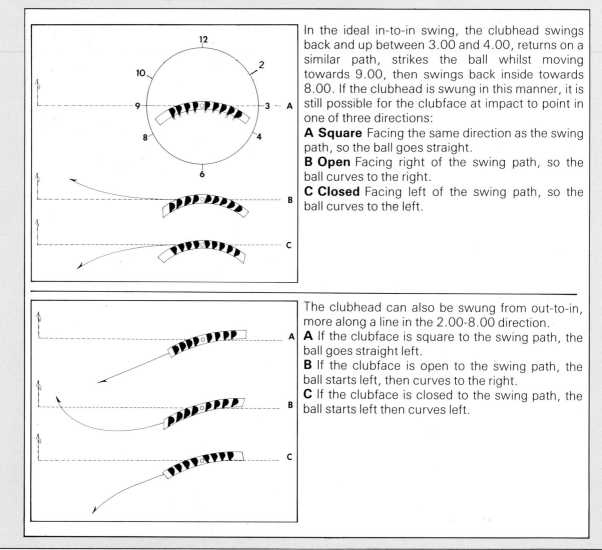

In the ideal in-to-in swing, the clubhead swings back and up between 3.00 and 4.00, returns on a similar path, strikes the ball whilst moving towards 9.00, then swings back inside towards 8.00. If the clubhead is swung in this manner, it is still possible for the clubface at impact to point in one of three directions:
A Square Facing the same direction as the swing path, so the ball goes straight.
B Open Facing right of the swing path, so the ball curves to the right.
C Closed Facing left of the swing path, so the ball curves to the left.

The clubhead can also be swung from out-to-in, more along a line in the 2.00-8.00 direction.
A If the clubface is square to the swing path, the ball goes straight left.
B If the clubface is open to the swing path, the ball starts left, then curves to the right.
C If the clubface is closed to the swing path, the ball starts left then curves left.

The clubhead can also be swung from in-to-out, more along a line in the 4.00-10.00 direction.
A If the clubface is square to the swing path, the ball goes straight right.
B If the clubface is open to the swing path, the ball starts right, then curves to the right.
C If the clubface is closed to the swing path, the ball starts right, then curves to the left.

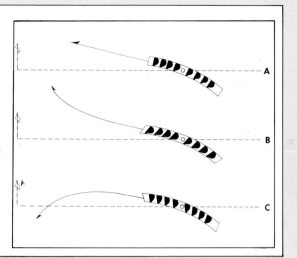

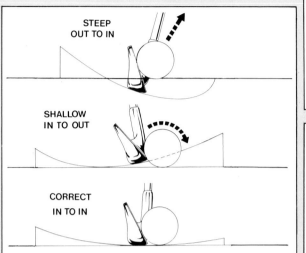

The angle of attack

Because you stand to the side of the ball, and not directly above it, the swing path should be from in-to-in. As the ball is not at eye level but on the ground, there is also an up-and-down element to the swing. This is called the angle of attack, and is very much a product of the swing path.

The out-to-in swing path creates a steep attack, directing most of the force downwards. This is suitable for some short game shots because it creates considerable backspin, giving height. But it is not the most suitable angle of attack for longer shots because length is lost.

The in-to-out swing path creates a shallow attack, directing most of the force of the swing forwards. This can be acceptable for shots from a tee, but makes hitting crisp iron shots more difficult. This is because in extreme cases the lowest point of the arc is likely to occur behind the ball, so that it is struck whilst the clubhead is ascending, resulting in a topped or thin shot.

The in-to-in swing path creates the best angle for all long and many of the short game shots. It provides a good balance of forward and downward attack.

You'll be pleased to know that to be a better golfer, you do not have to commit these facts to memory, but do refer back to them when necessary. By being able to analyze your own mistakes, you can then put them right.

Why more golfers slice than hook and how to correct it

The correct hand action, which squares the clubface at impact, can be hard to achieve at first, and usually the clubface remains open at impact, sending the ball spinning out to the right. To counteract this result, the golfer then starts to swing to the left, using the powerful-feeling right shoulder area, and neglecting hand and arm action. Sadly this only adds fuel to the fire, because now there is an out-to-in swing path with a very open clubface which creates a vicious slice, where the ball starts left then veers alarmingly to the right.

Slices, hooks and other imperfect shots

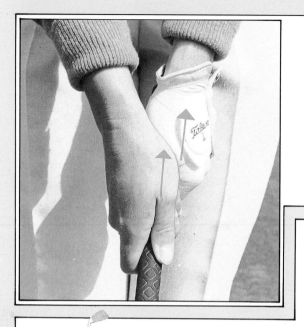

To correct this first check your grip. If both 'V's' point too much towards the chin or to the left of it, then move both hands to the right, so that the 'V's' point between the right side of the face and the right shoulder, as on page 17. Do not grip too tightly. Next check your aim and ball position. It is likely that the ball is too far forward in your stance, and your shoulders aim too much to the left. Refer to pages 30-33, which show the correct set-up.

To improve your hand action, and with a firm but not tight grip, choke down on a short iron. Stand with your feet close together, and swing your arms back to waist height only, allowing your wrists to fully cock. From this point swing the clubhead to a similar position on the through swing. You are trying to achieve clubhead speed by developing good *hand action*, which so far has been lacking in your swing. Notice that in each picture, the butt end of the club points to the ground. Do this at first without a ball, just trying to clip the grass.

A good exercise for developing the correct inside attack is to stand with the right foot drawn back, placed almost directly behind the left. Swinging from this position it is easy to keep the clubhead on the inside and it promotes improved arm and hand action. It is difficult to use the right shoulder area. The reason an inside approach to the ball is essential, is because it is only from this direction that the clubhead will be travelling towards the target at impact. From an outside path, it would be travelling to the left of the target. An inside approach will also help to draw the ball — make it curve slightly from right to left — and this is important for female players, as it adds distance.

You also need to be more aware of swing path in the impact zone. Lay two clubs on the ground, one near your feet parallel to the target line, and the other just outside your clubhead along the 4.00-10.00 line. Practise swinging the clubhead parallel to this club, and it will help you cultivate a better swing path. You will probably feel that your arms now swing flatter, ie more behind your head than above it.

Once you have practised these drills to correct your slice, try to keep a very clear mental image of swinging the clubhead along a 4.00-10.00 path, while you are playing. This will counteract your old 2.00-8.00 line. You will *feel* as though you are swinging to the right of the target. As you continue to practise and improve, your mental image of the swing path will become more finely adjusted. But remember that the alterations you actually make, will be far smaller than those you feel you are making.

Slices, hooks, etc.

Curing the hook

The hook, that starts right then curves too far left, tends to be a more advanced players' problem. These players are likely to have developed good hand action which, if not timed correctly can close the clubface at impact, causing the ball to curve to the left. To counteract this, they then aim to the right, so the ball is hit on an in-to-out path with a closed clubface which produces a hook. To cure it, you need to check the grip and set-up, then your swing concept.

You will probably be aligned to the right of the target, with the ball too far back in your stance, thus encouraging too much of an in-to-out swing path. Re-align yourself parallel to the target, as on page 30, and move the ball forward.

If your grip looks like this, where both 'V's' point near to or outside the right shoulder, move them to the left until they point between your chin and right shoulder, as on page 17.

You need to visualize the clubhead swinging back and approaching the ball much more from the 3.00 o'clock direction. You can practise by putting another ball, or some tee pegs, on the ground approximately on the 4.00 line, then trying to swing the clubhead outside them. You could also use the same drill as on page 93, but angle the club more towards 9.00 rather than 10.00 as a corrective measure. You will now probably feel that your arms swing more upright, ie more above your head than behind it.

To encourage leg action that may have been lacking, and to help you feel how your hips should be starting to open through impact, set-up with a fairly narrow, but very open stance. When you swing you will feel the space into which your arms can swing after impact. This will increase your chances of keeping the blade square a little longer, instead of snapping it shut.

Shanking

A shank occurs when the ball is hit from the area on the club where the hosel and clubface join, ie the shank, causing the ball to shoot viciously to the right. The player often believes that she must have hit the ball off the toe for this to happen, but more often than not it has been hit from the other end of the clubface. The most common way to shank is by swinging very much from out-to-in, which pushes the clubhead out beyond the ball. The golfer who shanks in this manner will also fade or slice the ball, so re-read the part of this section on curing slices, making the appropriate changes. You may also shank because you set-up with too much weight on your heels, and then fall forwards towards the ball due to the force of the swing. So check your weight is distributed between your heels and the balls of your feet, and that with a medium iron you have at least a fist's width between the butt end of the club and your thighs (see page 23 *below*). Now practise the following drill.

Place a tee peg in the ground, then address it opposite the middle of the clubface. Now swing, and try to miss the tee peg on the inside. In doing this you are training yourself to re-route the clubhead down on an inside, instead of an outside track by approaching the tee peg from the 3.30 rather than the 2.30 line. To perform the drill successfully, you must remain balanced throughout, and not fall forwards. You should also sense more action from your arms and less from your right shoulder.

The other way to shank is from an exaggerated in-to-out swing path, where the clubface is left wide open. First check that your shoulders are not aligned too much to the right. Then take the clubhead back initially on the 3.00 o'clock path, keeping the back of your left hand facing the target. The inside shank often happens because the player rolls her hands open. On the downswing keep your head very steady, so that you don't get ahead of the ball before impact, and try to make the toe of the club reach the ball before the heel. You will have a greater sense of your hands and arms rotating anti-clockwise through impact.

Topped shots

A topped shot occurs because the ball is struck above its equator, which creates top spin causing the ball to travel along the ground.

This shot can be caused by the fact that the radius of the swing, set at address by the left arm and shaft, has not been completely restored at impact, so the ball is struck above its equator. The reason for this is often due to too tight a grip, which stifles hand action. The drill for improving hand action in the slicing section would be a good remedy (see page 92). Place your hands on the club so that they feel firm but not tight, then try to maintain that pressure throughout. Hitting shots with your feet together is also beneficial.

Experiment with the ball position; it could be too far back, or too far forward. By making a few swings without a ball, you can easily see where the club contacts the ground. Position the ball just before this point for iron shots, and progressively further forward for the fairway woods and driver. It is important to remember that for crisp iron shots the clubhead must be descending; often a player will try to help the ball into the air by hitting *up* on it. Imagine another ball immediately in front of the object ball, and try to swing the clubhead down through that as well.

Some ladies hit up on the ball because they are afraid that taking a divot after impact requires outstanding strength. This is not true; it just requires a good free swing of the clubhead, and the correct picture of it descending onto the ball, with your weight moving towards the target.

The beginner may top or thin the ball because she fails to maintain the angle of the spine set at address. Instead, during the backswing the body raises up with the arms (as on page 62), and so the radius of the circle has increased, and you may miss the ball altogether. Keep your spinal angle constant, and your head the same height, until well after impact.

If your mechanics are fairly sound, topping and thinning may be due to poor timing. Re-read the section on timing on page 69.

Fat shots

A fat shot occurs when the clubhead contacts the ground before rather than after the ball. The true power of the shot is lost and, depending on how much turf is taken, the ball will not travel very far.

The radius of the swing is completed before the clubhead reaches the ball. To cure it you need to put a little more emphasis on pulling down with the left arm, and creating more leg action by moving the left knee laterally towards the target. This will help to move the base of the arc forwards, so that you strike the ball first, then take a divot. You should feel that you pull the clubhead back to the ball, rather than throw it from the top of the backswing. Re-read the section on timing.

Fat shots can also be caused by having too much weight on the left leg at the top of the swing, then transferring it to the right side of the downswing (see page 63, top).

Be sure to transfer enough weight onto the right side in the backswing, even if initially you feel that you are swaying a little.

Chapter 3

The short game

This is the part of the game where the women can be as good as, if not better than, the men because for the majority of shots in the short game, strength is not of prime importance. Instead, a vivid imagination and a good touch are of the essence. With long shots, you merely select the club that hits the ball the required distance, but in the short game, clubs are not specifically designed for shots of say 30 yards, or 43 yards; it is up to *you* to produce the required length. In order to do that successfully, you need to be able to visualize the shot before you select the correct club, and then execute the stroke.

This section explains how and where to play several of the shots in the short game, but the variety of shots at your disposal will increase with experience. Bunker shots and putting are also explained in detail, since proficiency in these departments will quickly lower your scores. Do try to spend at least 50 per cent of any practice session on all aspects of the short game work, it is the least tiring and most rewarding way to practise.

The short game

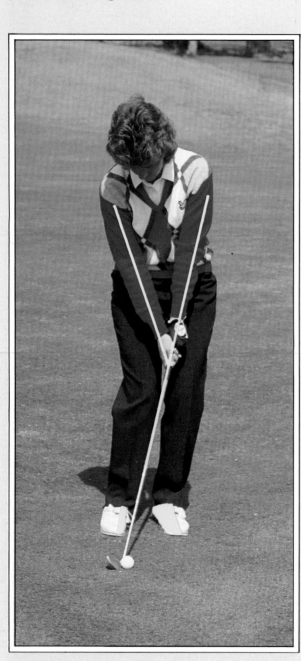

The chip and run

When you are just a few yards off the green you should play a low chip and run shot. Gripping down on the club, set-up with your shoulders parallel to the target line and adopt a narrow open stance, with your weight about 70/30 in favour of the left side. Position the ball well back in the stance quite near the right foot, but keep your hands ahead of the clubface, so that the shaft slopes towards the target. You can clearly see how my arms and the club form a letter 'y', and that my head is ahead of and not behind the ball. This set-up should guarantee that the ball is hit correctly with a slightly descending strike. The backswing is made by swinging the 'y' to the right, mainly using the forearms. This keeps the clubhead fairly low to the ground, and it swings just to the inside. There is very little movement in the wrists, and the weight remains on the left side. On long chips the right wrist may break a touch more.

The throughswing shows that my left wrist has remained very firm, and the 'y' shape is still intact. The clubface has not closed as in the full swing, because my hands have remained ahead of it, just as they were at address. My right knee has eased towards the target. The ball was struck whilst the clubhead was slightly descending.

The short game

Most poor chip shots are hit because of a bad set-up, and this shows the most common fault. The ball is too far forward, and the hands and weight are too far back. From here I am almost guaranteed to hit a fat or thin shot.

This is the outcome: the backswing was made purely with the hands, and now the right hand tries to scoop the ball into the air on the upswing. The back of the left wrist has buckled, providing no support.

This is a good practice drill. Set-up, then grip another club as shown. If you swing correctly, the second club shaft will not hit your side. If you swing incorrectly, you will soon tire of hitting yourself, and be keen to improve! The correct feeling is very much one of dragging or pulling the clubhead back to the ball, keeping the hands ahead of the clubface all the time.

This action should be used for all chip shots, regardless of which club you use. Try to make the swing rhythmical even though it is very short, and keep the backswing and throughswing the same length. The correct movement, for players who have been using too much independent hand action, will feel rather wooden and rigid. Some golfers like to feel that they are tossing the ball onto the green with the right hand, and that image might work for you, but *always* keep the back of your left wrist firm through impact.

Your choice of club will depend on the situation, and to some extent on your preference. The better and more experienced golfer is instinctively able to use a variety of clubs, from the sand wedge to perhaps a 4 iron, in any given situation, but the novice would be better off choosing just two clubs, a 7 iron and a wedge. By restricting yourself to these, you will quickly become familiar with the strength of shot needed for various occasions, and you will find it easier to decide which club to use. When you hit a chip shot, ideally you should try to land the ball just on the green, and let it run up to the hole. You land it on the green because it is a smooth and even surface, so there is less likelihood of getting a bad kick. However, if the fringe is smooth, and the ground is not soft or muddy, the higher-handicap player and the beginner may find it preferable to use the 7 iron instead of the wedge. The point is, a badly hit 7 iron will not be as disastrous as a badly hit wedge.

Chipping from rough

When the ball sits in the rough around the green, you must make a steeper backswing to avoid catching the club on the grass. Keep the ball well back in the stance and hit down and through. The ball will come out low and run more than usual. If you need height, use a sand iron, open the face of the club and your shoulder line, and cut across the ball, aiming to hit the grass about 1–2 inches behind the ball. This is rather like a bunker shot without sand.

The short game

◀Imagine that the ball is 5 yards off the green, and the pin is 15-20 yards on. You could then use the 7 iron because, as a general rule, a chip with the 7 iron will spend about one-third of its journey in the air, and two-thirds on the ground.

◀If the ball is 10 yards off the green, and the pin is 5 yards on, the wedge would be better, because a shot with this club will spend about two-thirds of its time in the air, and one-third on the ground. Obviously clubs with more loft send the ball higher, which means that it does not run so much.

This gives you a good idea of how the ball reacts with different clubs. But bear in mind that shots will vary according to the ground conditions.

Some more advanced players and many professionals often prefer to use just one club, usually a wedge or a sand wedge, and by varying the position of the ball and the angle of the clubface they can produce a range of different shots. However, it is a good idea to learn how the ball reacts with different clubs, starting first with just two, and then progressing to others.

The short game

The long chip and run

It would be wrong to assume that every time you are too far from the green to chip, you should play a high pitch shot. Very often you can produce a lower shot that lands on the fringe or green and runs up to the pin simply by expanding the chipping action.

The stance is a little wider than for the short chip, but the weight still favours the left side, and the swing is very similar. The club is swung back mainly with the forearms, so that the clubhead initially keeps fairly low to the ground. As the ball is struck, the right hand rolls over the left a little, which will help the ball to roll on landing. This is the best shot to play when the pin is on the top of a two-tiered green.

The short pitch

1 This is the shot to play when you need more height on the ball, eg when you have to loft the ball over a greenside bunker. The set-up is similar to that for the chip and run, with the shoulders parallel to the target. The weight only just favours the left leg, and the ball is slightly further forward in the stance, so the loft on the club is more effective. The hands are just ahead of the ball, with the shaft sloping a little towards the target. Choke down on the club for added control.

2 Swing your forearms up so that the clubhead rises quite steeply. You do *not* need to employ a lot of conscious wrist action; your wrists will cock naturally. There is little weight transference onto the right leg, but the head remains very steady.

3 The forearms swing down, with the hands *leading* the clubhead back to the ball. No attempt should be made to help the ball into the air, as the loft on the club will do that nicely, if you let it. It is important to keep the clubhead square through and after impact, so that the ball gets maximum height and backspin. Your legs must work through towards the target to create good rhythm and to enable you to keep the clubface from closing.

4 You can see clearly that my right hand has *not* rotated over my left, but my arms have swung very much to the left side of my body, which is now facing the target. Try to keep the left hand and arm in control with this shot, so that the back of the left hand faces more towards the sky at the finish. The backswing and throughswing should be virtually the same length, which will help to create a good rhythm.
 The swing should feel quite firm, and arm-orientated. For many players I suspect this will feel rigid or wooden because — as with the chip shot — most poor pitch shots are due to too much independent hand action. So concentrate on swinging your forearms up, and keeping your hands fairly passive.

The short game

Varying the height and length of the short pitch

In the pitch, the clubhead is swung in a 'V' shape, creating more height on the shot, whereas in the long chip and run it swings in more of a 'U' shape, creating a shot that is lower. Therefore, you can vary the shots you play simply by thinking of the shape of the swing. Further variety can be obtained by changing your set-up. In the previous sequence I set-up with my shoulders parallel to the target line, and consequently swung from in-to-in, but by aiming yourself further left, and opening the clubface varying degrees, you can create an infinite number of shots. I would suggest you practise from the square position, then gradually open your stance, shoulder line and the clubface, so that you then swing from out-to-in, creating a higher softer shot. This way you will start to learn how the ball reacts, and how hard to hit it. I should also add that you can use the sand wedge for these shots, and this will send the ball higher since it has more loft. The only time when you should not use it is if the lie is tight, as the flange on the sole of the club will most likely bounce off the ground and you will thin the shot.

Also practise hitting the ball with a variety of differently paced swings, and you will notice that if you have quite a slow swing with a slightly open stance and clubface, the ball will fly high and land in a lifeless manner. This is called the lob shot, and the key is to keep the backswing and downswing at the same pace, making sure that you swing through the ball. This may be easier for the middle- to lower-handicap range player, but higher handicaps should at least practise it.

The more advanced short pitch

For some pitch shots, the lower-handicap player may like to use a swing that has slightly more wrist and hand action than in the pitch shot already described. This means using a conscious wrist break almost from the start of the backswing, creating a slightly steeper out-to-in path. This method does require better timing than the one I have previously described, as you will be using more independent hand action, but provided you swing your forearms back as well, rather than lift the clubhead up purely with your hands, the more experienced player may be able to develop a better feel. The ball will tend to go a little higher than with the more passive hand action as you will be creating slightly more backspin.

The long pitch

This shot is used from perhaps 60 yards out and beyond, and sends the ball mainly through the air, stopping quite quickly when it lands. The correct action will impart a great deal of backspin, which is what makes the ball stop quickly.

The set-up is basically the same as that for the long chip and run, with perhaps a little more weight towards the outside of the left foot. The swing is like that for any full wedge shot, with the arms swinging upwards quite steeply, and the wrists cocking quite early. There is less shoulder turn than for longer clubs.

On the downswing the left arm pulls the club down, and the hands must stay ahead of the clubface. At impact the left hand and wrist *must* resist the power of the right hand, as it provides a definite strike, helping to create additional backspin. It feels like a punching action, where the arms stop quite quickly after impact, but the right hand does *not* roll over the left.

The real beginner may find this precise action quite difficult to start with, and she should be quite content with hitting a simple wedge shot (as described in the section on full swing), which will stop the ball reasonably well. The more experienced player will gain that extra bite on the shot with the action described here, but do not imagine that the ball will suck back on the green as you may have seen it do for the top professionals. To get that kind of result, you need to be playing on receptive greens, to have a perfect or slightly tight lie with no grass between the clubface and the ball, and to be far enough from the green to hit the ball hard. You also need to be using a soft-covered Balata ball for the best results, and I would not recommend that for the vast majority of golfers (more about that later).

Varying the height and length of the pitch

As with the short pitch, the more you open your shoulders and the clubface, the more height and less length you will get. You can also vary the ball position; forward for more height, and back for less. Experiment using the sand wedge, wedge, and 9 iron, with a variety of set-ups and lengths of swing, as it is only by practice that you will discover all the options. Don't always think that you have to hit the ball very high to stop it, especially if you are playing into the wind. By putting the ball back in your stance, thus delofting the club, and by hitting perhaps a 9 iron instead of a wedge, you can hit a lower shot under the wind that stops quite quickly after landing. But do remember one important point: short irons are not made to be thrashed, they are designed for accuracy, and you are far better off hitting a controlled 9 iron than trying to force a wedge, only to miss the green.

Which shot when

I said at the start of this section that visualization is essential in order to become a good short game player. Some of the situations that you will encounter will offer you a choice of shot, and you must opt for the one that feels right, and which you are most capable of playing.

● Avoid the temptation of always taking the wedge out of the bag and trying to pitch the ball through the air just because your partner does. What suits her may not suit you.

● Certainly for the beginner and higher-handicap player the maxim should be: don't chip if you can putt the ball, and don't pitch if you can chip it. It is easier to putt than chip, and easier to chip than pitch.

As you progress, you may favour one shot or club, but do practise using different clubs and actions. You can often visualize the shot better by examining the situation first from the side. Work out how the ball needs to travel, whether the air route looks better than the ground, or vice versa.

Once you have pictured the shot, then select the appropriate club, have a couple of practice swings to help you judge the length of swing needed, then set-up, still using an intermediate target about 1 yard ahead to help you aim the shot. Play the shot using the same length swing as the practice swing, keeping your head very steady. Try to make the ball finish just past the hole — that is if it doesn't go in. By learning to attack with these shots, you may be surprised how many more you hole than with a more cautious approach.

Bunkers

Bunker shots are among the most dreaded by many club golfers, but really, playing the ball out of the average bunker, even from a less than perfect lie, is *not* that difficult, once you have learnt the correct technique. The difficulty lies in becoming a proficient enough bunker player to get the ball consistently within 1-2 yards of the hole. If you learn how to play the basic shot well, you will lose your dread of bunkers, and will undoubtedly progress from there.

Here are the most common faults that I see ladies make in the bunker:

1 They do not take a long enough backswing. Seeing that they have only a short distance to cover, they make a short backswing, failing to take into consideration the resistance offered by the sand.

2 Often as a result of taking too short a backswing, they fail to hit through the ball, and instead the clubhead 'dies' in the sand.

3 They try to hit the ball *up* in the air, instead of trying to take a divot of sand.

If you recognize any or all of these points in your game, then fear not, help is at hand, and you can improve.

The sand iron

The sand iron has been designed to help you play bunker shots. It is the most lofted club in the bag, with a flange on the sole that is lower than the leading edge. This prevents the clubhead digging too deeply into the sand, instead helping you to take a shallow divot of sand from around the ball. The more you open the clubface, the more the flange comes into play, causing the leading edge to sit further off the ground. Flanges vary in depth, and ideally you need one that best suits the sand you play from, ie deep for bunkers with deep powdery sand, and shallow for bunkers with little, or firmly packed sand. Many professionals carry several sand irons to suit the varying conditions they encounter, but of course you need not go to that extreme. Instead I would suggest that you check with your local professional that the particular sand iron in your set best suits you and your course.

The extra metal in the flange does make this a heavier club than the rest of your set, so if yours feels too heavy for you to control, consider getting a lighter one.

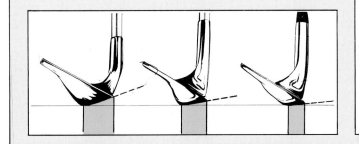

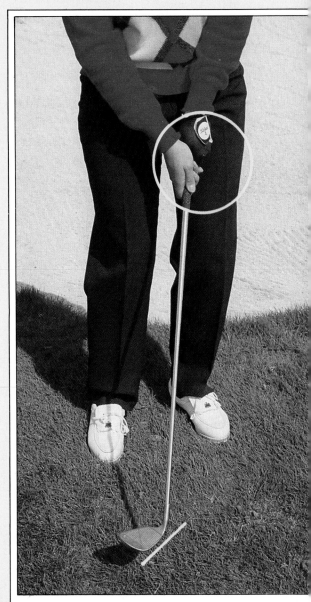

The basic splash shot

1 Before you grip the club, first turn it open about 20-30°, then take your normal grip. This helps to ensure that at impact the clubface will be open. This is essential to get height on the shot, and to make good use of the flange. Do not make the mistake of gripping the club squarely, and then opening it, as it will merely return to the ball in a square position. So: open the club first, then take your grip, choking down slightly for extra control.

2/3 Set-up so that a line across your shoulders aims about 20-30° left of the target. Wriggle your feet into the sand for stability; to help you strike down, wriggle the left one a little deeper than the right. Adopt a narrow open stance, with the weight favouring the left foot. The ball should be further forward in your stance than for a shot from

108

2

3

4

the fairway – opposite your left heel or instep – and your hands should be about level with the ball. Focus quite carefully on a spot in the sand about 2 inches behind the ball, because this is where you want the clubhead to enter. Also, hold the club above this point, not in behind the ball. If you think of the clock face, with the target at 9.00, the clubface aims at about 9.30, while your shoulders aim at about 8.30. This will automatically enable you to swing the clubhead steeply across the ball from out-to-in with an open clubface, thus creating height and spin.

4 The backswing is made by swinging the arms *up*, and allowing the wrists to cock naturally. You can see how the clubhead has swung outside the target line, as a result of my set-up.

Bunkers

5

6

6a

The basic splash shot

5 There is little weight transference or shoulder turn, and the club shaft points parallel to my body line, ie left of the target.

6/6a/7 The clubhead enters the sand about 2 inches behind the ball, and continues through to take a shallow divot. The right hand does not turn over the left, which must stay in control throughout the shot. My weight is now mostly on my left side, and my right knee is moving towards the left.

8 Please look at this picture and file it in your memory if you need to improve your bunker play. So many bad bunker shots are executed because the player fails to swing *through* the ball, but quits on the shot leaving the clubhead buried in the sand. You should finish with your body facing the target, weight mainly on the left side. The ball will fly on a fairly high trajectory, and will not roll much on landing.

When practising bunker shots, draw a line in the sand to represent the entry point, and without a ball just practise taking a shallow divot of sand about 6-8 inches long, from that point forwards. This encourages you to think about hitting through the sand instead of hitting at the ball.

On the course, it may help you to imagine that the ball is sitting on a £5 note, or dollar bill. Try to remove the area of sand beneath the note, and the ball will go with the sand.

The best bunker players never rush either their

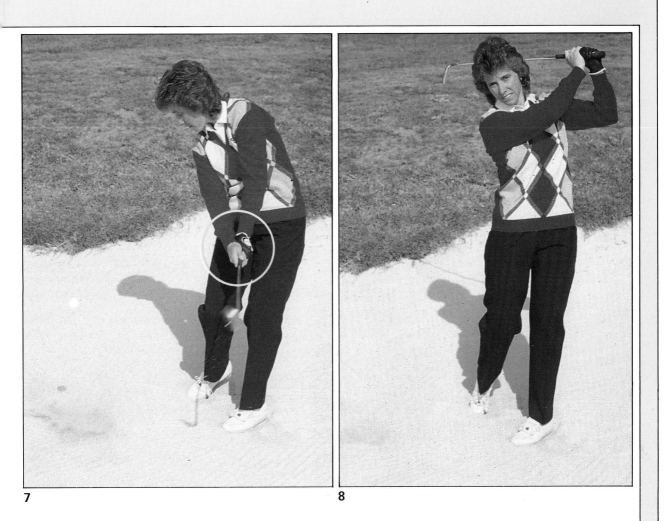

7   8

preparation, or the shot, so mimic them. Try not to get flustered, take your grip, perhaps outside the bunker so that you do not accidentally touch the sand with the clubhead before you have hit the ball, which would incur a penalty. Then still outside the bunker, have a practice swing to decide how hard to hit the ball, and to get the feel of the swing. Take the correct stance, focus intently on that spot behind the ball, then try to make a smooth unhurried swing, finishing as I have. Remember, all you are trying to do is to remove a divot of sand from around the ball, and the ball will go with it. Your first goal is to get the ball out first time, in the direction of the pin. Do not worry too much if it goes past or finishes short — the right distance will come with practice.

Varying the distance

There are several ways of varying the distance of bunker shots, but the easiest is to keep the entry point in the sand and your set-up constant, and to vary the power of the swing, just like you would for a pitch shot from the fairway. When you reach the limits of this system, you can open the club-face and your stance to give the ball more height and less length, or square the clubface and your stance to make the ball lose height and gain length. One word of warning: when it comes to very short shots, be certain to swing the clubhead through the sand. It is easy to take too short a backswing, and this will not give you enough momentum to complete the shot. The sand offers great resistance to the clubhead, so you must have enough speed to swing through it.

The best players in the world are able to assess each shot, and by a combination of changes in set-up, power and entry point, can produce almost perfect results. So if you start from the set-up recommended, perhaps swinging your hands back to shoulder height, you can use the result of that swing as a guide.

Bunkers

Plugged lies
Naturally you will not always find the ball in a good lie, but by making one or two alterations to your set-up, you should still be able to get the ball out of the hazard.

For the basic splash shot, the clubface is turned open so that the flange prevents the clubhead from digging too deeply into the sand. But when the ball is plugged, it is sitting lower in the sand than normal, so the clubhead has to penetrate deeper. The answer is to play these shots with the clubface and your set-up square, and the ball back in your stance. Keeping your weight favour-ing the left side, you then swing your arms up steeply, and hit down sharply about 1 inch behind the ball. Because the clubhead is penetrating deeper into the sand, the follow through will be curtailed. The ball will come out lower than with the splash shot, and run on landing. When the lie is less than perfect you may not always be able to aim at the pin; instead be content with getting the ball out, even if it is sideways or backwards. You *must* let the situation and your ability dictate how to play the shot, and always aim to get out first time.

Firmly packed sand
It is difficult for the clubhead to penetrate hard sand, so again keep the blade square, or only a little open, so that the flange does not bounce off the surface. Play the ball more centrally than for the splash shot, and make the entry point nearer the ball. Again with the weight on the left side, concentrate on hitting *down* very firmly through the shot. If you still lack success with this shot, try using your wedge, as its sharper leading edge will cut through the sand more readily.

Ball plugged in bunker face ▶
If the ball is plugged in the face of the bunker, there are two ways of playing the shot, depending on how best you can take your stance and keep your balance. You can lean *into* the slope, open the clubface a fraction, then hit into the slope as hard as you can about 1 inch behind the ball. You will not be able to follow through very much, but the ball should come out, even if it does not go very far. Alternatively, you can lean *away* from the slope, as in the uphill lie, then hit firmly into the sand about 1 inch behind the ball. This stance means the club has more effective loft, so the ball will go higher.

Uphill lie

Position your spine at right angles to the slope, with the weight on the lower foot and the ball nearer the higher. Then swing the clubhead along the contour of the sand. The configuration of the set-up will add loft to the club, so there should be no problems in getting height on the ball; in fact you may need to put more power into the shot to get the distance needed.

Where the severity of the slope prevents you setting-up in this manner, you will have to lean into the slope to keep your balance. Open the clubface, then hit very firmly about 1 inch behind the ball. Because of the bank of sand, you will not be able to follow through very easily.

Bunkers

Downhill lies

The downhill lie can present more problems, since effective loft will be deducted from the club-face, and invariably you will need to get the ball up quickly to clear the face of the bunker. You could overcome this by opening the clubface very wide, but that brings the flange into maximum effect, making it more difficult to penetrate the sand behind the ball. It is usually best to compromise by opening the clubface a little, but the ball will inevitably come out lower than usual. If the bunker face is very deep, it may be better to aim sideways even, or backwards, so that you get out in one shot rather than plugging the ball in the face of the bunker. Set-up as for the downhill fair-

way shot, with your spine at right angles to the slope, and more weight on the left foot and the ball back in your stance. Your left shoulder will feel much lower than usual. You will have to cock your right wrist almost immediately to avoid hitting the sand behind the ball. The clubhead must strike *down* firmly about 2 inches behind the ball and you should endeavour to swing *down* the slope, allowing your right knee to work through the shot. Do *not* be tempted into trying to hit the ball up into the air. No one finds these shots easy, but don't be over-ambitious: look for the easiest escape route, and hit down through the shot. The ball will come out lower and run more than usual.

Bunkers

Fairway bunker shots

If you have a long shot from a fairway bunker and the ball is lying well, you must first decide which club to use. It is essential that you balance ambition with reality, and avoid the risk of hitting the·bunker face. Look at the shot from the side, so that you can see quite clearly how quickly the ball must rise to miss the bunker face. This factor, and not length, must be the criterion for your club choice. Take into account that you will be playing the ball a little more centrally, so effective loft is deducted from the club. So if your first instinct is to use a 7 iron, be safe and take the 8, then you will be confident that you will clear the face. In fact I like to open the club just a fraction, just to be on the safe side. The set-up is square, with the ball further back in the stance. Work your feet into the sand just a little for stability, and choke down a similar amount on the grip — this will help you to catch the ball cleanly, and also firm up wrist action. Then make your normal swing, trying to hit the ball cleanly from the sand. With this shot, even a few grains of sand taken before the ball will dampen the effect, so you may find it helpful to get a clean contact on the ball by looking nearer the top of it rather than at the back. Do not rush the swing, make it three-quarter paced, and stay down with the shot a fraction longer than usual. If the ball is lying well in a shallow fairway bunker, perhaps nearer the back than the face, you could quite safely use a fairway wood, perhaps a 5 or 7. Just use the same routine as for the iron shots, and swing smoothly.

If the ball is lying down in the sand, use nothing more than a 7 iron. Set-up with the clubface and your body open, your weight favouring the left side, and hit *down* about an inch behind the ball. This is almost like a regular bunker shot, but with a longer club. Use the guidelines above to select the club.

Sidehill lies

When the ball is above you, grip down the club, play the ball more centrally, and stand a touch more upright. Because the swing will be flatter, the ball may not have as much backspin as usual, so it will run a little more on landing. Aim further right than usual to allow for the tendency to pull the shot.

When the ball is below your feet, you must bend more from the waist, increase your knee flex, grip at the end of the club, and above all stay down through the shot. Set-up fairly square to the target, because your posture will in itself promote an out-to-in swing path. Difficulties occur with this lie, because you will often have to stand with one or both feet out of the bunker, or even kneel with one leg in order to play it. Always have a couple of practice swings, obviously not touching the sand at any time, and check that you will be able to maintain your balance. If this seems unlikely, you may have to play an alternative shot, perhaps in another direction.

Putting ... a game within a game

I am often asked if it is possible to teach someone to be a good putter. The person asking this question is usually quite convinced that it is *not* possible, perhaps believing that it is ordained in the stars whether or not you will hole consistently from three feet. Whilst I would not claim that I can make everyone hole from this 'knee-knocking' distance without fail, I am convinced that my putting method would improve the standard of the vast majority of club golfers. The putting principles I advocate are those that many of the world's best putters incorporate into their game. Again it is a matter of getting the set-up right, and letting that dictate the stroke. Most poor putters set-up in a manner that encourages too much independent wrist and hand action, which is the ruination of most putting strokes.

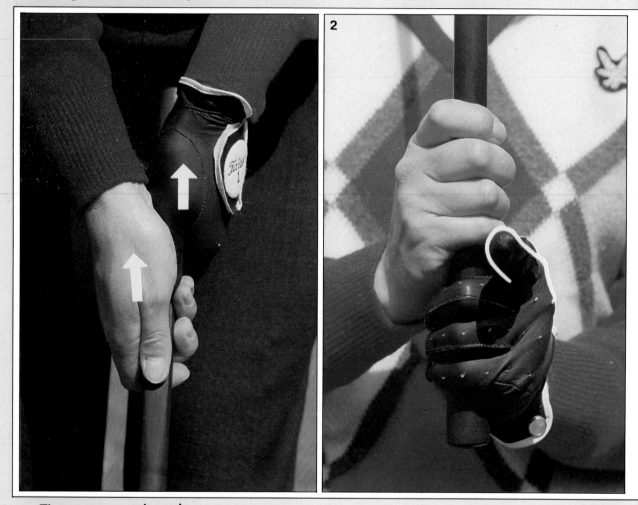

The reverse overlap grip

I strongly recommend that you use the reverse overlap grip, or a version of it, since it promotes stability in the back of the left hand and wrist.

1 With the putter face and your hands square to the target, grip the club with both hands completely on the club. Both thumbs will be at the front of the grip, and the two 'V's' must be more vertical than for the normal golf grip. The butt end of the grip sits more towards the middle of the left hand, rather than under the heel of the hand as in the normal golf grip.

2 Now remove your left index finger and slide the two hands together, overlapping the left index finger over the right hand.

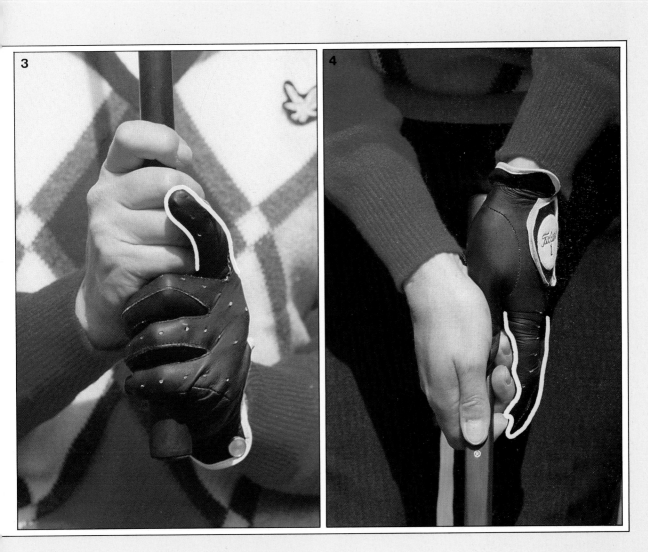

3/4 You can either extend this finger over all the fingers on the right hand as I have done, or just overlap one or two.

For players unfamiliar with this grip, it will feel strange at first, but I assure you that with a little practice it will soon feel comfortable. How tightly you grip the club is largely a matter of preference. Since you are trying to keep unwanted hand action out of the stroke, I advise a firm, but not tight grip. However, many of the top professionals prefer to grip the club very lightly, to get a better feel. The choice is yours, and only by experimenting will you find the best grip pressure that suits you.

Putting

In this set-up I have the putter face, my stance and shoulders square to the target line. I have bent forward from the hips so that my arms have freedom of movement. Both elbows are bent, but some people prefer to have theirs a little straighter. This is purely a matter of personal preference. My wrists are slightly arched, which helps to stabilize them, keeping hand action to a minimum. You may decide to putt with your feet open or closed; either is acceptable, but I would recommend that you keep your shoulders parallel to the target whichever way you stand.

My eyes are directly over the target line: to test this I am hanging the putter under my left eye. If your eyes are slightly inside the line, that is acceptable, but too far inside the line, or anywhere outside it, means you should adjust the set-up or ball position.

My stance is fairly narrow, but personal preference may mean yours is slightly different. Whichever way you stand you need to feel anchored, with the weight fairly evenly distributed, perhaps on the inside of the feet for added stability. My head is behind the ball, which is played just inside the left heel so that it is struck at the base of the arc or when the putter head is just on the way up. My hands are ahead of the clubface with the back of the left hand ahead of the ball.

Putting

The backswing is made by the hands and arms moving away together, so that the angle set at the back of the wrists at address remains constant. This ensures that the putter head stays close to the ground, moving just to the inside as the length of the putt progresses.

It is essential that the wrist angle should remain intact through impact and beyond, as this will ensure that the putter head does not get twisted off line, and that it stays close to the ground. You may find it helps to think of the whole of the grip moving towards the hole. As a result the ball will roll smoothly across the green. My head and body have remained very still, and will continue to do so until the ball is well on its way.

These two photographs show the path of the putter head. It is only on very short putts that it moves straight back and through, but as the length of the swing increases it has to move inside the line on the backswing, although not quite as much to the inside on the throughswing.

Putting

The action to avoid

Here the hands are too far back at address, but this is only a mild example of the fault. Severe cases, where the hands are almost opposite the right thigh, cause the shaft to slope quite noticeably away from the hole, instead of slightly towards it.

The incorrect set-up causes a stroke that has too much independent hand and wrist action. While the hands have moved considerably, the arms have remained almost stationary. Therefore the angles at the back of the wrists have changed. Compare this to page 122, left.

The result of the wristy backswing is a wristy throughswing, where the back of the left wrist collapses inwards instead of retaining its original angle and providing firmness in the stroke, as in page 122 right.

This action makes consistent striking, and judgment of distance impossible.

Putting

Try left below right

A good way to improve the firmness of your putting stroke is to practice with the left hand below the right. This almost guarantees that the back of the left hand will remain firm throughout the stroke. Some top players, most notably Bernhard Langer, have some considerable success putting in this manner on the course.

Putting practice

Putting is largely about good touch and feel, but this cannot be developed without consistency of strike. This putting method will promote a solid strike. Practice short straight putts to start with, aligning the ball opposite the sweet spot on your putter (this is usually marked with a line), then smoothly accelerating the putter through the ball. Keep still until the ball has finished rolling, or hopefully has dropped into the hole. Practise these short putts to a hole through a track formed by two clubs laid parallel on the ground. Gradually increase the length of the putt, and increase the length of the swing.

To develop a smooth putting action, try to keep the putter face in contact with the ball as long as possible. On very long putts you may need a little wrist action to help create enough clubhead speed, but be certain to keep the back of the left hand firm through impact and beyond.

I putt using mainly my forearms; others say that their right hand provides the feel and the left the guidance. You must experiment to find what gives you the best results, and it may well be different from one game to the next. If I have been missing putts on the left, I correct it by making my left hand and arm more dominant in the stroke; if I have a spell of pushing the putts, I concentrate more on making my right hand and arm move towards the hole. These thoughts may work for you, but if not, you will find out by experimenting how best to improve.,

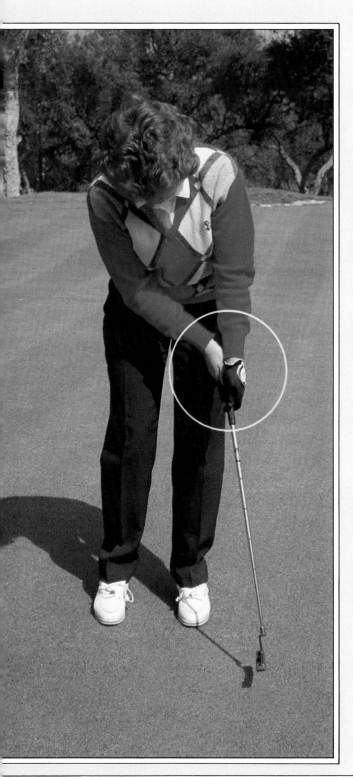

Judging distance and reading greens

Once you can consistently strike the ball from the middle of the putter, judging distance becomes less difficult, if not entirely easy. This is where visualization is important, and you must learn to become observant.

● As you walk towards the green notice which way the land lies; if you are walking uphill or down, the green is likely to slope the same way. From such observations you will learn how the ground will affect your putt.

● You should also take notice of the grass on the green. It can vary from hole to hole, being longer and thicker on some than on others. On faster greens the slopes will affect the putt more, and vice versa.

As you walk to your ball, ideally on the longer putts, you should look at it from the side so that you get a better idea of the exact length of the putt. From behind the ball the length of putt can be foreshortened. Remove any stones and mend any pitch marks on your line. Also try to feel through your feet whether you are walking on level or sloping ground, it is not always obvious to the eye.

To read your putt, crouch down behind the ball, looking towards the target, noting the height of the ground about a yard either side of the hole, because it is the slopes in this area that will have greatest affect on the ball as it loses pace. If you have a short putt that has borrow, you must decide whether to hit the ball firmly and fairly straight, or to hit it softer and allow for more borrow. Perhaps uphill you should opt for firm and straight, since if you miss the hole, the ball will not go far past. On tricky downhill putts, it is usually better to hit the ball softer, and allow for maximum break.

When you have assessed the line on which the ball must start, pick a spot on the green about two or three feet ahead over which to aim. Have one or two practice putts looking at the hole, and trying to visualize the ball rolling across the green and dropping into the hole.

Putting

Good visualization is one of the most important ingredients of becoming a good putter. I have made practice putts where I could 'see' the ball dropping into the hole so distinctly that I knew I had only to make a good stroke and the putt was mine. You too can develop this imagination if you start now, and be determined to see the ball dying into the hole with each practice putt.

One further piece of advice: whatever routine you adopt for reading putts, do not become a slow player. If it is not your turn to putt first, read the green at the same time as the other players if possible, so that you're ready to putt when it is your turn. I do not advocate putting into a circle around the hole, I think this is too negative. You should try to hole every putt, although I accept this might not be realistic for beginners and high handicap golfers, especially on long putts. Nevertheless, try to get into the habit of being confident. You may hole very few long putts, but you will never know what you might aspire to if you do not set your sights high enough.

There are also one or two exceptions to the rule. On some longer putts you may decide to leave the ball just short of the hole to avoid leaving yourself a tricky downhill putt back, for instance. Matchplay tactics may also dictate that aggressive putting is not called for at a particular moment. These instances are exceptions, and as a rule you should be trying to hole everything.

On longer putts, watch the ball as it approaches the hole, and see which way it breaks. Often I see players who have hit a poor putt turn away in disgust. If they had been more observant instead they would have learnt something about the next putt. Also watch your partners putt. Imagine how hard you would hit their ball, compare that to their strike, and see if you would have judged the pace and line correctly.

● To become a good putter, first you need to develop a good technique that rolls the ball across the green.
● Then improve your sense of perception, and be observant.
● Never hit a putt until you have visualized it dropping into the hole.

Chapter 4

Playing your round of golf

When the reading and practice are behind you, it's time to get out on the course, and put into action all those things you've learnt. So how can you make the most of your ability?

Ideally you should always arrive in plenty of time for your round. If you leave yourself no time to warm up or swing a club prior to your round, your muscles will take at least two or three holes to loosen up, so don't get too concerned if you play them badly. If you do arrive with time to spare, either hit some shots, or simply have some practice swings, starting with a short iron then gradually working towards a wood. Take it gently; you don't want to pull a muscle. Spend some time on the putting green, and perhaps chip a few balls. Get your score card organized, and check you have enough golf balls, tees, pencils, gloves, a ball marker, a towel, and a pitch fork. If you can do all this, you will be able to approach the first tee in a calm manner, and give your full attention to playing your shot.

Planning your round

Planning your round

Golf is a game of strategy, and a matter of plotting your way round the course. Obviously the higher-handicap player may not be able to realize her plans as often as she might wish, but even the total beginner should try to think her way round. Before you hit any shot, you should think ahead and decide where you wish to hit the next shot from. This will be based on the layout of the hole, the pin position, and your ability.

On a par 4 hole where you can see the pin, the middle- and low-handicap player should decide whether she would be better off hitting her second shot from the centre, right, or left of the fairway, and aim her tee shot accordingly. If the pin is on the left of the green, probably playing your second shot from the right side of the fairway would be better, and vice versa. The higher-

Tee up on the same side as any hazard or out of bounds then you can hit away from it. Depending on your ability plot your route.

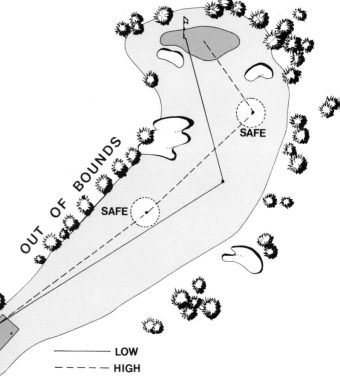

handicap player, who cannot reach the hole in two, needs to decide the best way of reaching the green in three, or even four. She may be better off playing a middle iron from the tee for safety, especially if the hole is tight. If there are bunkers to carry, and your best wooden shot always lands in them, then play short of them with an iron, until such time as you can carry them with confidence.

On par 5 holes, there are often two sets of hazards, set to catch the tee shot and the second, so a little extra planning is needed. Higher handicaps may not be able to get on the green in less than five shots; even so, try to plan the shot that will land on the green in advance. Middle-handicap golfers should make the green in three or four shots. Usually the only thing that will stop you is landing in a bunker, so try to aim away from them. Provided it is not too long, you would be better off in the rough than in a bunker. The lower-handicap player and long hitter must be looking to make par, or birdie the hole. It may be the time to risk a

Only the longer hitting low handicap player should risk a long carry, which may yield a birdie.

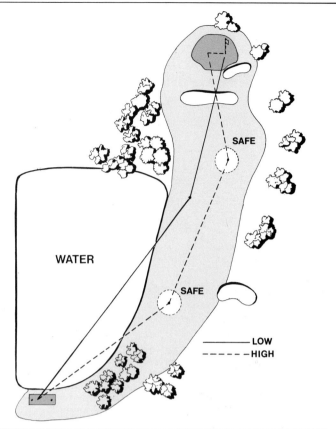

Planning your round

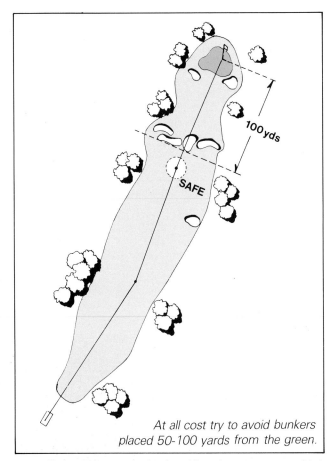

At all cost try to avoid bunkers placed 50-100 yards from the green.

miss the target to the right! Naturally with short clubs you will be more accurate, but nonetheless, it is always a point worth considering. So look at the pin position, and at the land around the green, and let both influence your next shot.

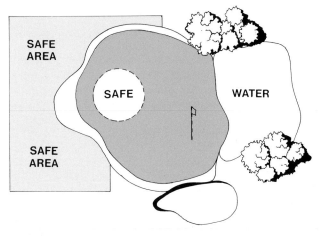

Consider which side of the green is the safe area.

little extra power in the drive, but you must think what would happen if the shot is not successful. If you are trying to cut off more of a dog-leg, or take the long carry over a lake, it could be disastrous if the shot fails, and the ball finishes deep in woods or water. If the fairway is quite open, and the hazards are negligible, then you can hit out with confidence. You then have to decide if the second set of hazards are a threat, or you can reach the green quite easily.

One of the hardest shots in golf is the middle-range bunker shot (from 50-100 yards), and often this is just where bunkers are positioned. If you are in doubt about carrying them, I'd suggest you play short, and rely on a good pitch shot. If you can easily carry them, note where the pin is, and also look either side of the green.

The fact that you still have a long second shot means accuracy is not guaranteed, and it may be safer to miss the green on one side rather than the other. Indeed, you should do this on most of your shots to the green; it is not being negative, just realistic. There is no point in aiming at the pin if it is just a few yards left of a pond, and you often

Once you are close to the green, you need to decide on a position to putt from, that is if you do not hole the pitch or chip! If the green is flat try to hit the ball hard enough to finish about a yard past the hole. If it is a very sloping green, try to leave yourself an uphill putt; avoid the temptation to attack if it will mean your next shot is a slippery downhill left-to-right putt. On the green use a similar strategy, but not to the point of becoming too defensive. There have to be times when you attack an uphill putt, but always try to leave yourself a short one back.

● All golfers have a handicap, and you should bear yours in mind when playing. Someone who plays off 36 has par values of 5, 6 and 7 on the course, not 3, 4 and 5. If you look at it this way, and try to incorporate the ideas I have already outlined, you will not feel as pressured, and will be better able to plan each hole, giving yourself an improved chance of beating your handicap.

To attack or defend
Every golfer needs to recognize the right time to attack the course. This will depend on:
● How you are playing that particular day.
● The lie of the ball.
● The punishment likely if the gamble fails.
● The state of play in your round or match.
Everyone's standard of play varies from day to day, and it is pointless gambling, or playing your normal attacking shots, if for some reason you are

playing badly. Just because you usually carry a distant ditch with a 4 wood, is no guarantee that you will make it if you have been topping the ball all day. Don't let your ego ambush your common sense; lay up short, so as not to be unduly penalized. You may enjoy trying to draw a certain shot around the trees, but if the ball is lying in the rough or in a divot, settle for something less spectacular, and save your shot-making ability for another time.

You must consider what will happen if the attacking shot fails. If you try to draw a ball, but it starts right and fails to curve, will it finish in the woods or just another part of the fairway? If you risk carrying a ditch, can you reach the green? If not, don't risk a penalty shot: you would be better off laying up short.

Some people are gamblers by nature and, despite the odds stacked against them, they will decide to play a certain shot. However, it is mainly men, because of their extra power, who want to

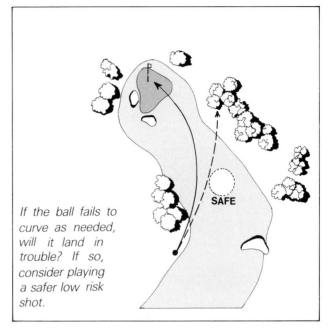

If the ball fails to curve as needed, will it land in trouble? If so, consider playing a safer low risk shot.

Is carrying a ditch worth the risk if you still don't reach the green?

Planning your round

play high risk shots. Often I point out the options to a player, trying to encourage them to play the safer shot, but the thought of pulling off a shot that Seve Ballesteros or Laura Davies would be proud of predominates and they opt for death or glory. Playing a better-ball format allows such a cavalier attitude, but when it is just your ball that counts, especially in medal play, judge if the situation warrants all-out attack, or whether being a little more defensive would be prudent. Ladies are much more prepared to play sideways if necessary, rather than trying to make up for a stray shot by attempting the almost impossible.

So before you decide whether to attack or defend, weigh up the situation, bearing in mind the four factors I have mentioned.

Club selection
Take care in choosing the club to play. If you play mainly at your home club it is easy to become complacent about club choice, especially at par 3 holes, where so often the same club is automatically pulled out of the bag without considering the pin position or wind direction. A little extra thought and time may make a par or even a birdie much more likely.

Consider the wind direction before automatically selecting your club.

Your partners' influence
Try to keep to your game plan, and don't be swayed by other people's play. Your three partners may all take out their drivers on a particularly tight hole, but even if they hit good shots, play a fairway wood, if this is what you had in mind. If you take the driver, the chances are you will doubt your choice, and will invariably hit a bad shot. However, there will be times when your partners' play can positively help you. If you see their shots land woefully short of the green, perhaps they have misjudged the strong wind that might be blowing, and you should adjust your club selection accordingly. This is not changing your game plan, but merely learning from other people's mistakes.

Concentration
Try to concentrate on each shot and don't let those that you have played, or those yet to be played, prey on your mind. If you have started the round badly, all is not lost, provided you forget those bad shots. You will derive great satisfaction from being able to play the rest of the round well, despite your discouraging start. Most golfers take a few holes to warm up and adjust to the conditions of the day. Professionals always take time on the practice ground to rid themselves of their bad shots, and if you have not warmed up prior to your round, then you should accept a few less-than-perfect shots to start with. There may be shots ahead of you that you dislike intensely, but by letting your mind wander forward to those, you will not be concentrating sufficiently on the shot in hand. So try to stay in the present, thinking of nothing but the hole you are playing.

Golf requires an on-off concentration, since it is almost impossible and indeed unnecessary to concentrate solidly for the three or four hours you may be on the course. You need to stay relaxed between shots, and if chatting whilst walking relaxes you, then by all means chat, but the moment you reach your ball or even just before, switch onto the shot in hand. First of all visualize the shot, and try to imagine yourself playing it. Select your club, have a practice swing if necessary, pick out your intermediate target, address the ball, then hit it. One point to add about talking on the course, is that your playing partner or opponent may prefer to play almost in silence. You may then find that quietly humming a tune to yourself helps you to relax.

Swing thoughts
I doubt whether any top class player hits the ball without a pre-conceived idea of how it should

Visualize the ball's flight before you hit the shot.

feel, or without a simple swing thought. In your pre-shot routine you should visualize the ball's flight and how your swing will feel to produce that shot. For the better player this is usually quite simple and fairly automatic. The middle- and high-handicap player may need more deliberation when, for instance, trying to draw or fade a ball, so use your practice swing as a rehearsal. If you are making swing changes, then you may need to be thinking about one or two points that you can work on while playing. This might be something in your backswing that needs altering, or simply an improvement in your tempo, but bear these points in mind throughout the round. If conscious swing thoughts distract you, just being conscious of the clubhead swing path through impact may help you to swing freely and produce good shots, and you can leave more complicated thoughts to the practice ground.

Some golfers play their best and swing with greater freedom just visualizing the ball's flight, rather than concentrating on any physical movement.

You must decide which is best for you, but you will probably be a better golfer if you learn to play the round with one appropriate swing thought in mind. It could help you to rectify minor swing faults even when playing a competition.

Develop tunnel vision to highlight your target and block out the trouble.

Planning your round

Being aware of the clubhead's swing path through impact may help you to swing freely and produce good shots.

The first tee

Do not rush your first tee shot. Find a part of the tee that gives a firm stance and smooth path for the clubhead. Visualize your shot, blocking out of your mind the parts of the course where you do not want to hit the ball. Try to develop tunnel vision, so that you get a strong narrow picture of where the ball will fly. Then check where to aim. Don't fall into the trap of always aiming in the direction in which the tee points, as they are often misleadingly built facing into the trees or across a fairway. Remember what I said in the driving section, tee up so that you hit away from any trouble. Pick your intermediate target about one yard ahead of the ball, and use that as your guide. If you are a very nervous player, especially on the first tee, take several deep breaths to relax. Prior to your swing, try to do everything in slow motion, because it is almost certain that you will be rushing around. Make sure you complete your backswing, and try to finish balanced. If the hole

136

The rules

is a par 4 or 5, do not automatically use your driver, especially if you haven't warmed up and the opening tee shot is a bit tight. Choose a fairway wood or even a middle iron that you can hit well, and then you are not putting pressure on yourself.

If you hit a poor shot, do not worry, it is not the end of the world, despite the fact that you feel that everyone was watching. Many golfers, especially beginners, are self-conscious. Most people who play golf are far too interested in their own game to be watching *you* very intently. Moreover, we have all had to learn the game and make mistakes. Locate your ball, then prepare to play your next shot, trying to incorporate at least some of the points made in this section.

The playing rules of golf are complex, but you do not have to commit them to memory. Everyone should carry a rule book, and know their way around it, especially where to find the lost ball, unplayable ball, water hazard, and obstruction rules, as these are the most frequently used. You can now get illustrated books and videos on the rules, which are helpful. Alternatively, ask one of the more experienced players in your club or, ideally, the professional about the rules you do not understand. Take time to read the rule book before the playing season starts, and whenever you have the chance, because by knowing the rules you can often help yourself, and avoid disqualification by inadvertently doing the wrong thing.

Etiquette

Apart from learning how to hit the ball, golf demands that you observe a code of etiquette, and you will be accepted by your club members more readily on your standard of etiquette than on your standard of golf.

Here are a few very important points that must be observed:

- Never talk, move or make a noise while your partner is playing.

- Stand so that neither you nor your equipment is in their vision.

- Do not swing near or towards other people.

- Do not walk close to others who are swinging.

- Be ready to play when it is your turn.

- Keep up with the pace of play.

- Call players through if you are looking for a lost ball, or they are playing faster than you.

- Do not hit until the group in front of you are out of range.

- Shout 'fore' when the ball is in the air, if you have hit it towards other people.

- When on the green, place your clubs at the nearest point en route to the next tee.

- Do not place your golf bag or trolley on the green.

- Do not tread on your partner's line on the putting green.

- Attend the pin for your partner.

- Walk carefully on the green, and repair any spike marks you make, after the hole is completed.

- Mend pitch marks and replace divots.

- Rake bunkers, or level the sand using your club and feet after hitting your shot.

- Do not throw clubs, you look stupid and it is bad manners.

These are the main rules of etiquette to observe, and are designed so that every player has the opportunity to play their best. You must always consider other people, and then we can all play in optimum conditions.

Exercises and practice tips

Golf requires a balance of strength and suppleness, and there are many useful exercises for improving both of these. The strengthening exercises will not turn you into a muscle-bound specimen; they will help you to control the club, and ultimately hit the ball further. Generally speaking strong arms and legs will benefit your game, because tiredness will impair your mental as well as physical ability to play. The more you play the stronger you will become, but there are many simple and effective exercises that you can perform at home, which over a period of time will improve your play. You must always guard against repeating an exercise too many times; as a general rule, little and often is best. It is easy to pull a tendon or a muscle, and then you would be unable to play golf at all until it was healed, so start with a low repetition and build up.

Warm-up exercises
These exercises should be carried out before each round and practice session, and prior to more extensive and energetic exercises. Always start slowly and gently, and repeat each exercise about five times.

1 Stand upright, with your arms out horizontally to the sides, and feet apart, then turn from right to left, and repeat. Start gently, then gradually turn a little further each way.

2 Stand upright, feet shoulder-width apart, arms hanging to your side. Bend sideways, stretching down to the right and then to the left.

3 Slowly stretch and circle your arms either side of your body.

4 Place your hands on your hips, feet slightly apart, then bend your knees, and keeping your back erect, lower yourself to the ground.

5 Standing upright, turn your head from side to side, until your chin is almost over each shoulder, or progressively as far as you can.

6 With your hands formed into a fist, circle them either way.

7 Hold two clubs (you may not be able to use the proper golf grip), then gently swing them back and through.

Hand- and arm-strengthening exercises

1 Squeeze a squash ball, or a fairly solid piece of foam rubber, in each hand, exercising the weaker hand more often.

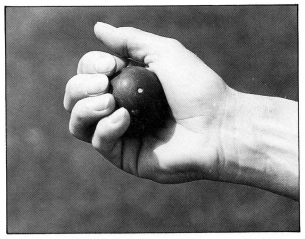

2 Attach a light weight at the end of a piece of string to a short piece of wood, perhaps part of a broom handle or some dowelling. With your arm held horizontally, palm down, wind the weight up and down. Repeat this exercise keeping the rod more in your fingers than in your palms.

3 Holding lightweight dumbells, sit with your forearms resting either on the arms of a chair, or on your thighs. Raise the weights up and down using your wrists and keeping your elbows and forearms still. This exercise should be done with your palms facing up and then down. If you do not have any dumbells, tins of food could substitute.

Exercises and practice tips

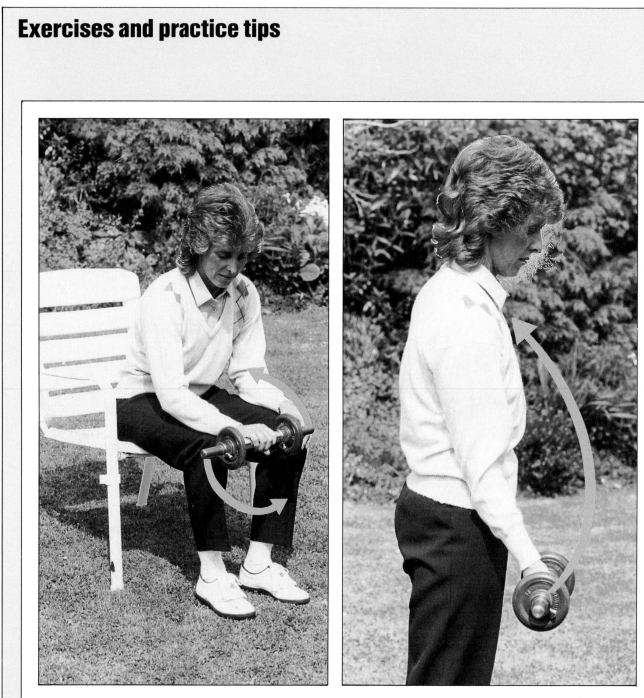

4 Sitting as in 3, hold the weights with your palms facing the ground. Rotate your hands so the palms face skywards.

5 Stand with your arms hanging by your sides, palms forward, and the dumbells in each hand. Bend your elbows, raising the weight to shoulder height.

7 Swing a weighted club, perhaps starting with just the head cover on one of your woods, then maybe progress by having some weight added to an old wood.

6 Swing a short or medium iron hitting through rough.

Exercises and practice tips

8 Choking down on a medium iron, grip it with your left hand only, but with the right hand on top of the left for support. Make half swings first, then increase the length. Stronger players can try this without the support of the right hand.

I have not recommended specific weights for the exercises, as this will vary from person to person. But the important thing is to start with a *comfortable* weight, and low repetitions, and gradually increase each.

Leg-strengthening exercises

1 Repeat the leg squats as in the warm-up exercise 4, increasing the repetitions, and then holding weights in each hand.

2 Cycling, either on a real cycle or an exercise bike, will improve the thigh muscles.

3 Skipping exercises the legs and hands, and improves your oxygen intake.

Any of the above exercises should only be carried out provided you have no physical problems that inhibit you, and to be safe, check with a medical expert first. Any time you feel too much strain, stop. If you can simply swing a golf club every day, even for just a few minutes, this will help to keep you supple, and gradually improve your strength.

I hope that you will devote some of your leisure time to practising golf, rather than always playing. It is only on the practice ground, or perhaps during a practice round that you will be fully able to commit yourself to any necessary changes in your game. Find a flat and even piece of ground, ideally sheltered from any wind, or with the wind blowing from right to left, as from this direction it is likely to ingrain good swing fundamentals. I have seen top professionals go to extraordinary lengths in order *not* to practise in a left-to-right wind, as this encourages a player to attack the ball from out-to-in. So be selective about where you practise, and give yourself good lies.

Always start by hitting a few short irons, not

Through practice your game will improve.

Exercises and practice tips

Practise in your garden pitching into an umbrella.

your driver, swinging easily, then gradually lengthening the swing. Most of your practice to change your swing should be carried out using a 5, 6, or 7 iron. These clubs are relatively easy to use, but will still reveal flaws in your swing, while the shorter irons tend to hide faults, and the longer clubs discourage good rhythm.

Work on one or two specific points or drills at each practice session, always integrating them into your full swing. What you must accept is that you may not hit the ball particularly well whilst making swing changes, however minor. Once you get over the uncomfortable feeling that any change inevitably brings, then you can concen-

144

trate more on the quality of strike. Also, spend some time practising overall rhythm, because when you practise specific parts of the swing, rhythm is usually affected.

Try to play shots that you will have to produce on the course. I once sat on the practice ground at the British Open and watched as one of the world's top professionals had his caddy call out different holes, and he would then hit the appropriate shaped drive for that hole. If your course has a specific shot that you dread or dislike, use your imagination and pretend you are playing that shot. Once you can play it well on the practice ground, you will overcome your negative feelings and do better on the course.

When you are over the initial learning stages, take time to pace out how far you hit the ball, ignoring shots you may have fluffed completely, or those that have gone several yards further than the rest. You may not have yardage markers on your fairways, but on all par 3 holes you will know the distance, and increasingly clubs are selling course yardage charts. Become familiar with how far you hit certain clubs, and that will help your judgement. Many shots can be saved by correct club selection, so do not neglect this exercise.

The better golfer should spend some time shaping shots, such as fades, draws, and high and low shots, with a variety of clubs. Also practise from a variety of lies, so you can learn which shots are possible, and how the ball reacts.

Always spend part of each practice session on your short game, as this is where most club golfers can quickly reduce their handicaps. Select your current worst short game shot, and try to improve that. Always try to finish your practice session with some putting, as this can represent about 50 per cent of your score. Short game practice can be done at home, indoors and out. You can chip and pitch in your garden either from the lawn, or a coconut mat, and try to land the ball on pre-determined targets. Putt indoors, preferably to a target such as a coin, that is smaller than the real hole, to make holes on the course seem a bigger target.

Make your practice interesting. It is better to hit 30 shots with thought, than a 100 not thinking about what you are trying to achieve. Use your pre-shot routine for each ball, don't simply keep dragging another ball over, without correcting your set-up. Try to practice to a target, maybe your umbrella, rather than a vague open space.

You might also find it helpful and more fun to practice with a friend, so you can encourage and help each other. However, a word of warning, don't blindly copy each other's swing changes. We each have different faults and need different corrections. If you have read this book and find a certain passage, photograph or drill that helps you, then persevere with it, even though it may not help your friend. Similarly, if you have a lesson, the professional will have geared the corrections to *your* faults, so keep to that advice, no matter if your friend has been advised differently.

Always practise with one or two clubs on the ground indicating the target and body line; top professionals do this, so copy them. Repeat your drills 5-10 times, and then try to incorporate them into your full swing. Most of the drills over-emphasize a movement, so if you overdo them, their value is lost, and they can become a fault in themselves.

I am a great believer in practising without the ball, as it is less inhibiting. Ideally do this using a mirror or glass doors to check your movements. I also think making shadow swings is very useful. By this I mean swinging without a club, just inter-locking your hands, to get a greater feel of exactly what your body is doing.

Endless hours are not required on the practice ground in order to improve, but some time spent even at home indoors can help you to correct your faults. When practising don't become impatient or too hard on yourself. Improvement tends to be gradual rather than drastic for most of us, and I know from experience that one's game can often get worse before it gets better. I have also made the mistake of practising a specific shot, and then expecting myself to hit it perfectly on the course. I was instantly putting pressure on myself, which made it harder to get good results. So don't expect instant miracles in this game; make long-term plans, and then you won't be disappointed. If you are someone who never practises then your improvement may be slow. Golf is such an exacting sport, that it requires work even from those with a sporting gift. I can assure you that every top player practises very hard, and whilst golf may only be your hobby, with a little extra effort you will undoubtedly get more enjoyment from this most frustrating, but exhilarating of sports.

Chapter 5

Your equipment

In chapter 1 I explained a little about equipment, focussing mainly on the differences between men's and ladies' clubs. You may not be able to buy success, but you can most definitely buy clubs that help or hinder you. Most ladies, and certainly most beginners, will not benefit from using men's clubs, but there are always exceptions to the rule. Those who may benefit are the stronger sports-orientated women who find ladies' clubs are so light they feel more like a set of wands. They will be better able to feel the clubhead in a heavier set, and will find heavier clubs improve their rhythm as well. No matter whether you buy ladies' or men's clubs, the following information should help you make the correct purchase.

The irons

I would strongly recommend that you buy a set of peripherally weighted clubs. This means that the clubhead has a hollowed-out back, with the weight distributed around the outside. It follows that there is a larger optimum area of strike (the sweet spot), and such a club could be described as a forgiving golf club, as it does not demand quite the accuracy of strike of the normal blade.

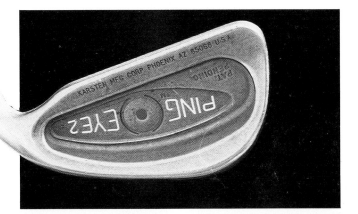

It is important that the lie of the club is correct for you. When you address the ball, the toe end of the sole of the club should be just off the ground.

If the sole rests completely on the ground, or the heel is off the ground, then the lie is too flat. At impact the toe end can catch the ground, leading to faded or pushed shots.

If the toe sits well off the ground at address, then the heel may catch the ground at impact, and cause pulled or hooked shots. Tall players generally need more upright clubs than short players, but your professional can adjust the lie to suit your physique. Most sets of irons are 3-sand wedge, but if you buy a half set, I would opt for the 5, 7, 9 and sand wedge.

Your equipment

The woods

It is possible to buy a separate set of woods to your irons, although having a matched set does give the advantage of uniformity. For all but the better player, I would not recommend buying a driver; instead, choose 2 or 3 wood, plus a 4, 5 and 7 wood. The 2 or 3 woods are more forgiving than a driver, and the little distance lost is worth sacrificing for accuracy. For those buying just a few clubs, choose a 5 wood to start, then add as you progress. Many golfers have found metal woods to their liking. They are a little easier to hit than conventional woods, because they too have peripheral weighting: they consist of a metal shell filled with a lightweight material such as polystyrene. Because of their weight distribution, they also tend to hit the ball higher than other woods, so that a driver with a loft of 10° might be more like a 13° wooden driver. They do not need as much care taken of them as wooden clubs, and this too has led to their popularity.

Graphite shafts and clubs

If you are prepared to spend a little more money, you could look at a set of clubs with graphite shafts, as these will give you additional length. There are now a great variety of these shafts made in several different flexes, so I would strongly recommend that you hit some shots with them before buying. Many female golfers find them ideal, as their slower, more rhythmical swing suits this type of shaft. You can also get graphite-headed clubs; these are claimed to hit the ball further, but do cost a lot more money than normal clubs.

No matter which set you choose, you must like the feel and look of them, and what suits one person may not suit another.

The less loft on a wood, the harder it is to hit.

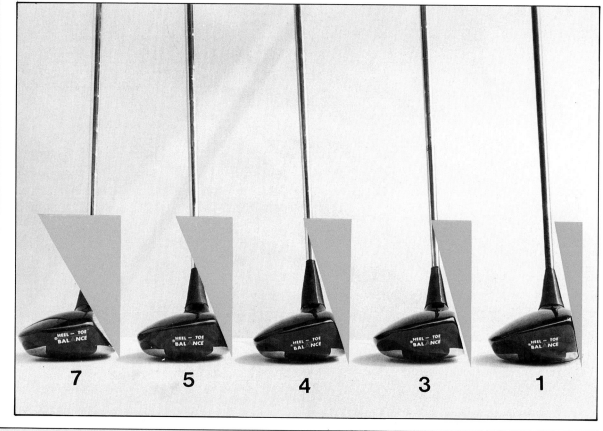

148

Club inspection

Although good equipment, correctly set up for you, is important for every player, once you gain a low handicap there is little room for error, and the right equipment is essential. Ideally, you should have the lofts and lies checked at the start of each season, because iron heads can and do alter slightly with use. Conventional woods are not always perfect, and may sit with the face a touch open or closed, so it will help you to know that yours are right for you. See that the grips are still good, first by giving them a thorough scrub with soap and water, then by replacing any that are too slippery and shiny. Shafts and whipping can start to come loose, so ask your professional to check them as well.

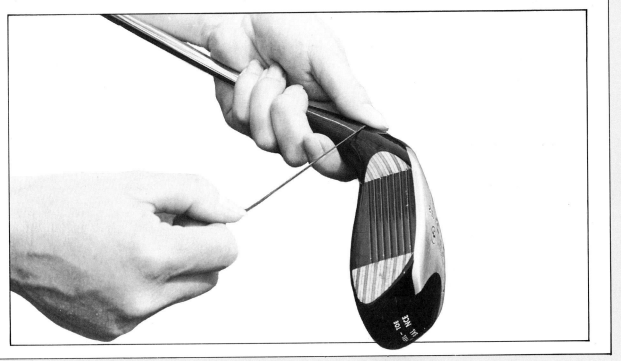

Your equipment

Putters

Putters are very much an individual preference, although I would strongly recommend a Ping or Ping-type, with heel and toe weighting that produces a larger sweet spot. If you find the shaft too long, have it shortened. This does change the feel to some extent, but it is more acceptable than having the grip catch on your clothes as you putt. Despite the fact that you may have seen some top professionals who putt with the toe of their club well off the ground, buy one that sits reasonably flat when you address the ball, or else you may catch the heel on the ground and twist the face off line. The lie can sometimes be altered to a certain extent, but not always, so keep this in mind when you choose your putter. The weight of putters varies a lot, and you will find that a heavier one is harder to twist off line, while you may derive more feel from a lighter one. It is quite easy for your professional to add weight to your putter, so try one that is medium- to lightweight, and then experiment if you are not happy with it.

Although all different in shape, these putters each have heel and toe weighting.

Golf shoes

A firm footing is essential for all shots, and metal-studded shoes give the best and most reliable grip. Regularly check that the studs are dirt-free, and not loose or worn, and replace them accordingly. Rubber-studded golf shoes are often more comfortable and lighter in weight, and are fine in most situations. However, if you play on a particularly hilly course, or in muddy or sandy conditions, your grip will be better assured with metal-studded shoes.

Golf gloves

Some people think that if you have never worn a golf glove, you never need one. But the glove is worn on the left hand — most people's weaker one — to give you a firmer and more secure grip, so for that reason I would advise you to wear one. Don't use a glove that has become worn and hard, because that will not help with the grip. If it gets wet, remember to take it out of your bag, and leave it to dry naturally. There is a good range of all-weather gloves, and you will find these last longer and are more versatile than leather gloves, so give them a try. Ladies often choose to wear two gloves to protect their hands, and whilst this is not necessary, if it helps you, then continue using two.

Golf balls

Golf balls are either wound or solid. The wound variety have a small inner core, around which is wound a long thin length of rubber. The surface is made of either Balata or Surlyn. Balata is the softer cover, and makes it easier to shape shots and spin the ball. This type of ball feels softer to hit, and is ideal for top professionals who usually hit the ball with the spin they want. The club golfer regularly hits the ball with unwanted side-spin, so this type of cover accentuates mistakes; moreover it marks very easily, so does not last long. The Surlyn-covered ball has a harder surface which is less susceptible to spin and marking, so opt for this cover if you buy a wound ball.

While the better player may find the wound ball has a softer feel, the solid ball will go further, and its harder and more durable cover is virtually cut-proof. The ball has an altogether livelier feel about it, which some players find more difficult to control around the green. But I strongly recommend that the beginner and middle- to high-range handicap player use this ball. Lower-handicap players may also find it to their liking, especially on long courses with soft greens.

Golf equipment continues to evolve, and today's latest clubs are tomorrow's cast-offs. It is fun to experiment with different clubs, and as one becomes better and more engrossed in the game, a new set of clubs can be a revelation. I know many ladies who, having started with a beginner's half set, have then invested in a better quality set, usually with peripheral weighting and often with graphite shafts, and have seen their game improve enormously. But do not think that you can only play with the most expensive set in the shop; get a set in your price range that suits *you*, ideally try them before you buy them, and progress from there.

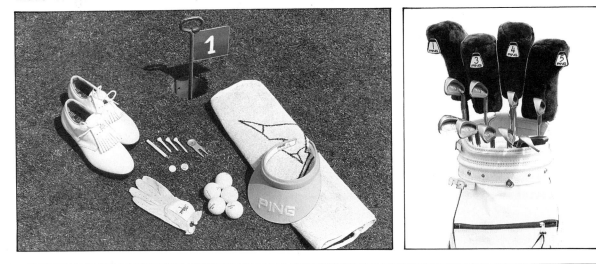

Glossary

Address

Backswing

Address The position the player adopts opposite the ball prior to swinging the club.

Angle of attack The angle at which the club approaches the ball.

Arc The curving path of the clubhead during the swing.

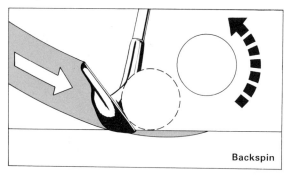

Backspin

Backspin The spin that causes the ball to rise; more evident with the shorter irons, which strike the ball low down. A driver, since it strikes the ball higher up, will impart little backspin, and more sidespin.

Backswing The movement of the clubhead away from the ball, until it changes direction and begins its downward journey.

Ball position The position from which the ball is played, usually related to and determined by the position of the feet.

Birdie A score at a hole that is one shot less than par.

Bogey A score at a hole that is one shot more than par.

Borrow The amount a player aims to the side of the hole to allow for the slope.

Centrifugal force The outward moving force present in rotary movement produced in the downswing.

Chip shot A low running shot from off the green.

Closed With reference to the stance, it means the player has aimed her feet, hips or shoulders right of the target. With reference to the clubface, it

Closed

Eagle A score at a hole that is two less than par.

Face The surface of the club from which the ball is struck.

Fade A controlled left-to-right movement of the ball in the air, caused by left-to-right spin, which tends to subtract length from the shot.

Fairway The closely mown area of the course between tee and green.

Flange The area on the sole of the club, particularly on a sand iron, which is lower than the leading edge, and adds weight to the club.

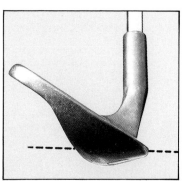

Flange

Downswing

means the face is aimed left of where it should be at address and in relation to the plane during the swing.

Divot A piece of turf removed from the ground by the clubhead, or the hole left by the removal of this turf.

Downswing The movement from the end of the backswing downwards towards the ball.

Draw A controlled right-to-left movement of the ball in the air, caused by right-to-left spin, which tends to give more length to a shot.

Drive The first shot on a par 4 or 5 hole, usually played with a wooden club, but not necessarily a driver.

Driver Sometimes called a 1 wood; the longest and least lofted club in the bag; used to gain maximum length.

Glossary

Flat swing When the club and arms are swung too horizontally.

Fluffing A completely mis-hit shot that travels very little distance, because the club contacts the ground before the ball.

Follow through The part of the swing after impact.

Forward press A slight forward movement often of the hands and right knee, used as a trigger movement for the backswing.

Fringe The area of closely mown grass around the green, between it and the fairway.

Green The very closely mown area on the course where the hole is situated.

Grip The rubber tubing on the shaft which the player holds. Can also refer to the actual placement of the hands.

Handicap The allowance given to each player referring to the average gross number of strokes in excess of the standard scratch score, in which they complete the course. Ladies' handicaps range from plus to 36, and men's from plus to 28.

Hazards Ditches, lakes and sand bunkers on the course.

Hook A sharp right-to-left movement of the ball in the air.

Hosel The part of the clubhead into which the shaft fits.

In-To-In This relates to the swing path through impact approaching from inside the target line and returning to the inside after impact, ie from 3.30-9.00-8.30 in clock face terms.

In-To-Out This relates to the swing path through impact approaching from inside the target line travelling towards the outside of the line, ie approximately in the 4.00-10.00 o'clock direction.

Lie This can refer to how the ball is sitting on the grass. It also refers to the angle between the sole and shaft of a club.

Loft The measurement in degrees from the vertical on the face of the club.

Match play This form of golf is where one golfer plays another on a hole-by-hole basis, as opposed to counting the total number of strokes.

Medal play This form of golf, also known as stroke play, is where every stroke played is

Open

counted, and totalled for each hole. Each hole's score is then added, resulting in a gross score.

Open With reference to the player, it means she has her feet, hips or shoulders aimed too far left. With reference to the clubface, it means it is aimed right of where it should be, either at address or in relation to the plane during the swing.

Out-To-In This relates to the swing path through impact approaching from outside the target line to inside; on the 2.00-8.00 o'clock line.

Par The official score set for a given hole depending on its length.

Pitch A high shot through the air that rolls little on landing. Usually played with the 9, wedge or sand iron.

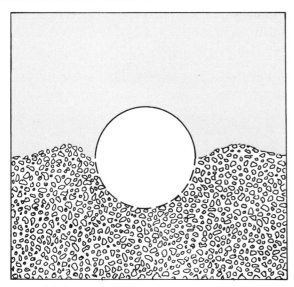

Plugged ball

Skied shot

Plugged ball A ball that rests in its own pitch mark on landing, so that some of the ball sits below the level of the ground, or sand.

Posture The angle of the back, and set of the hips, legs and head at address.

Prefered lies When a player is allowed to place the ball on the fairway, usually within 6 or 12 inches of where it lies, not nearer the hole. Often referred to as Winter Rules.

Pull A shot that travels straight left with no curve on it.

Push A shot that travels straight right with no curve on it.

Rough The areas of grass on the course that have not been closely mown, usually on either side of the fairway.

Set of clubs The maximum number you are allowed to carry is 14. This usually consists of 3 or 4 woods and 9 or 10 irons, plus a putter.

Set-up The same as the address.

Shaft These days the shaft of a club is usually made of metal or a carbon compound. The flex can vary from fairly whippy (an 'L' shaft), to regular (an 'R' shaft), and stiff or very stiff ('S' or 'XS'). The flex point in the shaft can also vary to give different flight characteristics and feel.

Shallow attack This denotes that the clubhead approaches the ball from a shallow angle to the ground, and is apparent with the driver.

Shank The part of the clubhead where it bends to become the hosel. Also the name given to the shot when hit from this area. The shot can also be called a socket.

Skied shot A mis-hit shot from the tee that, due to too steep an attack, is hit from the top edge of the clubface (usually a wood), resulting in the ball flying high, with little carry.

Slice A strong left-to-right movement of the ball in the air, resulting in loss of length.

Sole The base of the club, which rests on the ground at address.

Square With regard to the set-up, it indicates that the body and feet are correctly aligned parallel to the target line. When referring to the clubface, it means that it is at right angles to the target line, or to the swing plane.

Stance The position of the feet at address.

Steep attack The opposite of shallow attack; refers to the angle of descent of the clubhead to the ball.

Stroke The forward movement of the club with the intention of striking the ball.

Stroke play The same as Medal Play.

Strong grip This means that either, or both hands are turned too much to the right on the grip.

Sway Unwanted lateral movement to the right or left during the backswing or downswing.

Swing path This is the track of the clubhead during the swing, and is especially referred to when describing the path of the clubhead in the hitting area, in relation to the target line.

Swing plane The angle of the swing in relation to the vertical, best viewed from beside the player, looking towards the target.

Glossary

Square

Swing weight A system of measuring the balance of the club. Weights vary from ladies' clubs, about C3-C8, to men's from C9-D2, with the heavier end of the scale at D3 upwards.

Swing weight

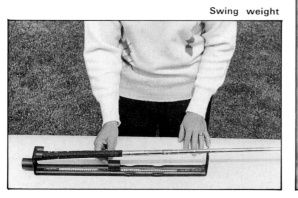

Target line An imaginary line from the ball to the target.

Tee The area of ground at the start of each hole designated for the tee shot. Also refers to the wooden or plastic peg on which the ball sits for the tee shot.

Through the green This is the area between the tee and green on each hole, excluding the hazards.

Tight lie When there is little grass between the ball and the ground.

Top This is when the clubhead strikes the top half of the ball, resulting in it travelling along the ground rather than in the air.

Upright When the arms and the club are swung too vertically. Also refers to the resultant plane of the swing.

Vardon grip Another name for the overlapping grip. Named thus, since it was Harry Vardon who first used it.

Waggle The back-and-forth movement of the clubhead at address, prior to the swing, used to dispel tension, and as a rehearsal for the correct backswing path.

Weak grip When either or both hands are placed too much to the left on the grip.

Wrist cock The upward hinging of the wrists on the backswing and through swing.

Wrist cock

Index

U

Uphill lies 84, 113

V

Vardon grip 18
Visualization 94, 128, 135-136

W

Warming up 138
Weak grip 21, 92
Wedge 24, 32, 101, 10ɔ
Weight distribution 48
Weight training 139-140
Woods 11, 71-79, 148

Acknowledgements

There are many people without whose help this
book would not have been possible. First, I must
thank my husband Ken, whose experience and expertise
in producing golf books, patience and guidance have
played a major part. My thanks go to Scottish
professional, John Stark, with whom I have worked
for many years. He has been a great influence on
my teaching, having been most generous in imparting
his knowledge of the game.

An especially big thanks goes to Karsten UK Limited
for providing me with their PING golf equipment. It has
been a privilege and a pleasure to be associated with
this company for many years, and their continued
support is much appreciated.

Several other companies have been kind enough to
supply me with clothes and equipment, so thanks are
due to Lyle and Scott for clothing, Stylo Matchmakers
for shoes, and Titleist for golf balls and gloves.

Grateful thanks to the directors of Wimpey Leisure
at El Paraiso Golf Club, Spain, to S. Ortiz-Patino
of Valderrama Golf Club, Spain, and to the Captain
and Committee of Thorndon Park Golf Club, England, for
the generous use of their courses for the location
photographs.